# LIVING WITH LOSS

# LIVING WITH LOSS

## *A Book for the Widowed*

Liz McNeill Taylor

ROBINSON
London

Constable & Robinson Ltd
3 The Lanchesters
162 Fulham Palace Road
London W6 9ER

First published by Fontana Paperbacks 1983

This edition published by Robinson Publishing
an imprint of Constable & Robinson Ltd, 2000

A copy of the British Library Cataloguing in Publication
data is available from the British Library

ISBN 1-84119-105-1

Printed and bound in the EU

# Contents

# Foreword to 2000 Edition

*Living with Loss* was my first book, written when I was working as a freelance journalist, and now, when I read it, I feel as if it was written about someone I used to know because life has moved on so much.

After it appeared, I went on to write four more non-fiction books as Liz McNeill Taylor – on bringing up children alone; living alone; making a living out of freelance journalism and twentieth century antiques – before starting to write fiction as Elisabeth McNeill.

My first novel, *The Shanghai Emerald*, appeared in 1987. Since then I have written twelve novels and am currently working on the thirteenth. I live in the country in a cottage with my pets and am supremely happy – something I would have found difficult to believe when I wrote *Living with Loss*.

My children, who play such a big part in the story, have been a continual support, joy and encouragement to me.

Pennie, my eldest girl, is a well-known Scottish journalist and broadcaster, specialising in health issues. She is the single-parent mother of my first grandchild, Rohese, who is about to go to university.

Sarah, who is married to an architect called Abe Odedina, is the mother of two girls, Iyunade and Okikiade. After gaining an honours degree in English, she went into publishing and is now editorial director for Bloomsbury Children's Books.

Eleanor, my baby, became an architect but branched into painting and illustrating. She illustrates books, designs cards, sells paintings and had one of her portraits chosen for exhibition in the 1998 BP Portrait competition.

Adam, my son, has roamed the world, starting off in Australia when he was seventeen, and going on to work as a trawler deckhand out of Corunna in Spain, plant trees in Canada, and then work on a sheepfarm in the Falklands. From there he went on to run an estancia in Patagonia. He married a Chilean girl and they have four daughters, Paulina, Mary, Dorothy and Valentina – there's a tremendous run of females in our family. They now live in Talca, about 200 kilometres south of Santiago, and Adam too is working on a book.

Printer's ink seems to run in my family's veins, perhaps because one of my ancestors started Mudie's Circulating Library.

# Acknowledgements

For all their help and advice with this book I would like to thank Mrs Dawn Robinson, Mrs Ena McPherson, Mrs Elspeth Walder, Miss Jean Smillie, Dr Brian Betts, Rev. J. Brown, Mr Francis Longstaff, Mrs L. Kosky, Dr D. Doyle, and the anonymous widows and widowers who talked so openly to me about their feelings and experiences.

For permission to reproduce copyright material I am grateful to the authors and publishers mentioned below.

Barbara Tuchman (Random House Inc. and Russell & Volkening): extract from *A Distant Mirror*.

Jenny Joseph (J. M. Dent & Sons Ltd): extract from the poem 'Warning' in *Rose in the Afternoon*.

Elizabeth Bowen (Jonathan Cape Ltd): extract from *The Death of the Heart*.

Maurice Lindsay (Paul Harris Publishing): extract from 'The Farm Wife' from his *Collected Works*.

Stella Gibbons (Curtis Brown Ltd): extract from *Cold Comfort Farm*.

Belsky (Times Newspapers Ltd): the cartoon on page 102.

# 1

## The Terrible Transformation

THE most significant day of my life was a Sunday, the day I attended the christening of the baby son of two of my friends. The ceremony was held in a church in the City of London and it was to be followed with a party at my friends' home near where I lived in South London. I never reached the party.

During my absence a policeman knocked on the front door of my home and told my mother that Adam, my husband, who was on a business trip to Singapore, had died in his hotel there. Though he was only forty-three years old he had suffered a sudden and fatal heart attack.

My distraught mother felt incapable of breaking this awful news to me so waylaid the baby's father to ask him to tell me what had happened. Before I started to write this book my memories of that first awful day of my widowhood seemed dim and confused. 'I can't remember much about it,' I told myself, but in fact this has turned out to be untrue. Once I forced myself to remember, the clarity and detail of my memories have been astonishing. Everything can be brought back in painful immediacy – the weather that November day, the slithery feeling of the leather-bound steering wheel of the car that I gripped when the news was broken to me, the taste of my tears and the racking pain in the chest that comes when sobs rise from deep down inside you. Most vivid of all is the memory of my utter disbelief in what was being said . . . disbelief and a terrible, numbing coldness.

The friend who had been asked to tell me about Adam's death climbed into the passenger seat of my car as I parked it at the front door.

'Sit still for a moment. I have something to tell you.'

I looked at him, surprised but totally unapprehensive. I thought he had forgotten something and wanted me to collect it for him. His face, however, was expressionless, as if it had been carved.

'Something has happened to Adam.'

Beneath my winter coat, I suddenly felt icy cold and the hairs stood up on my arms.

'An accident?' Even as I spoke, something told me it was worse than that. He stared back silently and in an effort to prevent him saying any more, I reached for the door handle.

'I'll go straight out there. I'll catch the next plane.'

I was desperate to stave off anything more from him but he still stared back and put his hand on the door to prevent my escape. I sank back into the seat.

'Oh God, you're not trying to tell me he is dead?'

'Yes, I'm afraid he is dead.'

The conversation only lasted a few seconds but so very few words were all that was needed to change my life completely, to destroy everything that had mattered most to me until then and to set me on a new path that was pitted with unexpected hazards. For the first time I was put totally in control of my own destiny. Whatever happened to me from then on was to be the result of my own actions and my own decisions. It was

like a terrible and painful rebirth with a ripping away of everything that had gone before and a cruel debouchment into a
dark future.

When the word 'dead' was first pronounced on my husband only half of my mind believed it. Even in shock it was
always hard for me to show emotion before strangers but now
I clung to this friend in an ecstasy of grief, weeping, 'He can't
be dead, he can't be dead. I loved him so much, you see.'

I became a sort of schizophrenic. Half of me knew it to be
true but the other half was seized with a strange ability immediately to fantasize the situation. I imagined that his passport had
been stolen and it was not my husband but the thief who lay
dead in Raffles Hotel. Cutting through protests, I insisted that
we telephone Singapore to check on the identity of the dead
man. I swept into the house, brushing everyone aside and told
my friend what he had to ask on the phone.

'Find out if he has blond hair. Ask if he has a mole on his
left foot.'

Forbearing to point out that Raffles Hotel knew Adam well
because he had been staying there intermittently for over a
year, my friend obediently made the call and of course it was
true that it was my husband who had died, though it took
weeks for me to accept the fact with the conscious part of my
brain and years to come to terms with it in my subconscious.

What made acceptance difficult for me was my long-held
conviction that if anything bad ever happened to either of us,
the other would be immediately aware of it. We were the sort
of couple that can surprise one another by the ability to pick
up and start discussing an idea that was running through the
other's mind. We sometimes had parallel dreams, an occurrence
also experienced by W. B. Yeats and his wife but apparently a

rare phenomenon in marriage. Yet I had failed Adam. I had sat happily through the christening ceremony when he was in his death throes and no twinge of apprehension had even touched me. Had I not loved him enough? How could he die without me knowing about it? I wondered if his last thoughts had been of me and the children, whether he had called out for me. I have never had the consolation of being given an accurate, first-person description of how he died – various accounts were relayed to me that differed in the most minute details but, like a detective, I seized on every variation. I was told he had died in his bedroom, in his bathroom, on the balcony. I suppose that whoever relayed the stories had thought that the minute details would be too harrowing or irrelevant – he had died in Raffles Hotel and that was all that really mattered, they supposed. But it is important for the bereaved to be able to go into minute detail about the death of some-one they love. They are not being morbid for they want to know as much as possible about something that matters a great deal to them. They want to know so much so that there can never be any dark corners in their mind's picture, no spectres lurking to terrify them.

I was told that when Adam felt the first pains of his coronary he had sent for the hotel manager who was a friend of his. A few weeks after the funeral, I wrote to this manager in the hope that he would give me a complete description of what had happened but I never received a reply. A few years later a friend on a holiday to Singapore called at Raffles and asked for the manager only to be told that he had long before returned to his native Australia. There was no one in the hotel who could remember a guest called Adam Taylor dying there. Hotels dis-like guests dying on the premises and are anxious to expunge the memory as quickly as possible. I had a mental picture of his body being taken privily away from his room so that the sight of it would not upset any of the other guests.

In time I received a death certificate from the Singapore Government – a flimsy scrap of paper like a parking ticket and even less informative. It was put in a drawer of my filing cabinet, an insignificant end for a man's life. One of my unfulfilled ambitions is to go to Singapore myself and seek out any information that might still exist about my husband's death.

The day of Adam's death was suitably foreboding, grey and overcast, the bitter end of November. Since then that month has always seemed of ill omen for us, a time when misfortune lurks round every corner. The children always hated November and for a long time they hated Sundays as well.

'I hate Sundays, everything bad seems to happen then,' said my eldest daughter, years after her father had died.

The shock of that Sunday seemed to fill our lives with unexpected fears. Even the clothes that I was wearing when I heard the news about Adam seemed to take on some aura of malevolence and though for years I was too hard up to spend money on new ones, it was impossible for me to wear the christening clothes again. The dress hung stiff and uncreased on a hanger and from time to time I would finger the skirt and wonder if it would be advisable to try to wear it but a primitive fear prevented me. I was sure that if I ever slipped that dress over my head some new disaster would engulf us all.

In the end I gave it away to a jumble sale and when it was handed over I felt freed from a terrible threat.

Adam and I had been married for fifteen years and three weeks when he died and we had four children: Pennie, aged nearly thirteen; Sarah, who was eleven; Adam, whose ninth birthday was a few days after his father's death, and the baby, Eleanor, who was two.

The phone call to Singapore had absorbed all my attention but once my initial hopes were dashed, I remembered the children and found them huddled together in the sitting-room. My mother, who was weeping quietly in the kitchen because she had been very fond of my husband, had not been able to tell them about their father's death. 'Your father is ill,' was all she could manage to say after the police officer left. When she saw me heading for the sitting-room, she tried to hold me back.

'Don't tell them, don't tell them,' she said, putting her hands on my arm but I shook her off. I *had* to tell my children; it was of supreme necessity for me as well as for them. I felt they were the only people who could most sincerely share my grief. There was also some inarticulated thought that it would be cruel and insensitive to tell them a mollifying lie only to have to contradict it later. They would have to know in the end and how could I mourn without them knowing what was wrong? My thoughts were chaotic however and as I shook off my mother's hands I was not acting from calculation and deduction but from emotion.

The sitting-room was dimly lit, the curtains half drawn against the grey mist of the garden. In a corner the television flickered with its sound turned down and the shadows of the room corners were so deep that someone could have been standing there watching us as I said, 'Your father is dead, darlings, he's dead.'

I began weeping again and we rushed together, clasping each other, arms entwined, the children clinging to my legs like kittens round a cat.

Today I think there is a closer bond between me and my children than there would have been if their father was still alive. Fierce is a strong word but it is the only adjective that fully describes the intensity of my love for them. A few years ago I attended the funeral of the husband of a close friend and was moved to tears by the sight of her and her four children sitting, shoulder to shoulder, in the front pew of the church. They looked as if they were physically joined together by what had happened to them – by touching each other and their mother they were providing mutual support and love.

Unfortunately my decision to tell the children about Adam's death was the last conscious thought I had about their feelings for a long time. My own grief stunned me and absorbed me too deeply to give much consideration to how the children were reacting and that was a failure on my part.

It was ten past four in the afternoon when I was told that Adam had died and now looking back it seems as if the rest of the day was aeons long. Every second was so full of feeling that I must have lived a lifetime in a few hours. Telephone calls were made to family and close friends – everyone had to be told the news twice because they found it difficult to take in the first time. My mother phoned the doctor to come to me because I think she feared I was going mad; a neighbour from across the lane somehow heard the news and came in through the unlocked back door with tears running down her cheeks. We had only been acquaintances before that day but wordlessly she walked up to me and folded me in her arms like a child. Somehow that calmed me, the sight of her tears helped me. Adam's closest friend Peter arrived. He too was weeping and again I felt comforted, knowing that I did not have to tell him how much I was suffering. My own closest friend, Lorna, arrived and said that she would stay with us till the funeral was over. Her calm stoicism and down-to-earth common sense were a great support to me through the black days that lay ahead.

It was very strange for me suddenly to find myself the centre of attention. People made cups of tea, pressed glasses of whisky into my hand, kept asking me if there was anything I wanted them to do. Never before had I been a ritual figure, for even at my wedding there had been no ceremony – we married on my afternoon off with only two witnesses in the church. My father did not like Adam and boycotted the wedding and Adam's mother, hurt by the fuss this had caused, stayed at home as well. There was no reception, no ceremonial speech-making. Now, for the first time in my life, I was transformed into the central figure of a human drama – the weeping widow in her kitchen. It was a role I deeply resented and from which I tried to dissociate myself. I was strangely able almost to observe what was going on from outside my own body – I saw the weeping woman as if she was on a stage. This dissociation from reality made me numb and detached, able to talk distantly, to act capriciously and behave with childish unrestraint.

For the first time in my life I was to be totally indifferent to the effect I was having on other people. From childhood I had been acutely anxious to please and it mattered a great deal if people liked me or not. I had to be approved of and this made it difficult to put much value on my own opinions or feelings. Now suddenly I was free, I could not care less about the impression I was making. Though it was then only a passing phase, I can now see that the seeds of the freeing that started so wildly that first day have grown over the years until I have achieved a greater liberation within myself.

However, a chance remark from a sympathizer presented me with what seemed to be a tailor-made persona for the widow.

'You are a sensible woman,' I was told. 'You are going to be all right because you are so practical.'

In fact I am not practical at all. That was only my front to the outside world and within myself I knew that practicality was not part of me but I clung to the words as if they were a lifebelt. Here was the solution. If I stiffened my lip and strove hard I could perhaps survive this horror. I could perhaps develop the qualities that other people seemed to see in me. The doctor arrived with a bottle of tranquillizers and another of sleeping pills. He sat with me at the kitchen table, talked to me and helped with arrangements for drafting a death notice. As he was about to leave, I lifted the bottles of pills and rattled them to see how many there were.

'Isn't it unwise to give me so many?'

He looked very hard at me to see if I was play-acting.

'I think I can trust you to do the right thing. There are your children to think about and you are a practical woman.'

There it was again, my new widowed role. Would it have been better if I had broken down, threatened suicide and forced the doctor to hand me out the pills in nightly doses? As it was I could not allow myself the luxury of expressing my own feelings of inadequacy and my terrible searing grief. I could not give the outside world any glimpse of the desolation that lay inside me. I wanted to be approved of again as the ideal widow.

My first piece of advice to anyone who is widowed is *grieve* – grieve openly, with theatrical abandon if that helps. Pay no attention to other people's embarrassment, tear your clothes, pour ashes over your head or break all the crockery in the house, make a public exhibition of your sorrow rather than carefully putting it away like a dress on a hanger. The wails of widowing should not be bitten back because wailing inside cannot be stifled forever.

# 2

## Funeral Rituals

IT has become a cliché to say that death is one of the great unmentionables of our society, but like many clichés there is truth in it. Sex can now be discussed without embarrassment in all its manifestations and though we pride ourselves on having cast off old taboos, we have introduced a new one – we cannot accept mortality. The Victorian attitude to sex is now considered either reprehensible or funny – how could they clothe table legs in pantaloons, when the back streets of the cities were sordid stews and outwardly respectable men frequented the foulest brothels? In the same way as we feel superior to those attitudes we feel free of the Victorian morbidity and brooding on death. The Victorian children's book with some character always dying a pious death from consumption is now considered psychologically damaging. Instead we prefer to concentrate on the lighter side of life, on more hopeful things. Medical advances, heart transplants, miracle drugs encourage us to value the extension of life and close our eyes to the fact that in spite of all the wonders of modern medicine, we all must one day die. We are unable to consider the inevitability of death in the same way as our ancestors – trousered table legs and all – did. Aldous Huxley described the modern attitude to dying when he said, 'Most people behave as if death were no more than an unfounded rumour.'

As a child I was greatly influenced by my paternal grand-mother who was High Victorian in her attitudes. Our Sunday afternoon walk was always to the large city cemetery where my grandfather, her husband, had been buried thirty-five years before I was born. That graveyard was a place of fascination for me and also a place of horror. In those days graveyards were lovingly gardened and looked after – there were none of the overgrown and mournful burial plots that can be seen in cities today. It had a lilypond covered with waterlilies and full of enormous goldfish as well as rows and rows of graves, some very grandiose – monuments with red sandstone columns, marble busts, sorrowing angels and small children holding posies of flowers, surmounted by shrouded urns and hovering doves, carved wreaths and broken spears.

I practised my reading on the gravestones' inscriptions and can remember the thrill of primitive terror when it first struck me that real people who had lived, walked around and laughed just as I did lay beneath the stone slabs. John Donne slept in his shroud and kings and emperors in the past spent hours and much money planning their monuments and grave inscriptions, but all that seems unhealthy and excessive to us today. We are embarrassed that we have not been able to do any-thing about dying – man who can fly to the moon and dive to the bottom of the sea has not conquered death. Because people spend their time trying to ignore it, when death does touch them it has a more shocking impact.

Only a few religions still practise ritual mourning, among them the Orthodox Jews who hold a Shiva week in which the bereaved family stays in seclusion supported by friends and relatives. Everything is done for them – they do not even cook for themselves. The function of the mourners' friends is to encourage them to grieve and to listen to them while they do so. For the majority of Western people, however, the emphasis in mourning is to make it as palatable as possible – to 'cheer people up' and to dispose of the dead as quickly, efficiently and hygienically as possible. The less fuss, the better the whole operation is thought to be concluded. Excessive emotion must be avoided at all costs – not only is it upsetting for everyone involved but it is also bad taste.

The mourners in crematoria are hustled through the services like cattle through a pen and they most obligingly connive at the unseemly haste with which the people they love are shuffled off this earth. One group of mourners is already queuing at the chapel door while those inside are leaving. It is not uncommon for people to sit through the wrong service unaware that they have joined in with someone else's funeral.

My own close experience of death had been when my father died after a long illness about five years before Adam. The perfunctory ceremony in the crematorium chapel was over so quickly that I was still sitting in my pew, convinced that there was more to come, while everyone else was filing out and I had to be nudged into leaving. It seemed utterly wrong that a life so full of incident and excitement as my father's could be terminated with only a few stereotyped words mumbled over his coffin by a clergyman who did not even know the name of the man he was burying for I saw him crane his neck to read the name on the coffin plate half-way through the address.

I was determined that Adam's life would not be terminated in the same unceremonious way – he must have a 'proper funeral'. When I was a child there had been what I thought of as a proper funeral in our home village – everyone in the community walked to the graveyard behind the coffin which was carried slowly along on a cart drawn by two horses. I remembered too how I used to tease Adam about his affection for India while we were living in Bombay, where we had spent the first ten years of our married life.

'If you stay in this country much longer,' I told him, 'you'll have to be burned in a funeral pyre on the banks of the Ganges when you die.'

If he had died there I could imagine how appropriate his burying would have been. I remembered funeral stretcher-bearers running through the streets in the early morning – the body stretched out with its face uncovered and wreaths of flowers and silver paper round its neck. Later from the burning-ghats near our house, a trickle of white smoke would rise up into the blue sky and I knew that round the funeral fire would be the family of the person who had died, keening their grief and throwing sticks of sandalwood into the flames.

Isolated among strangers in South London, however, I had little idea of how to organize a suitable funeral for Adam – I only knew there had to be one for only then would my mourning really begin.

Because his had been a sudden death and he had not consulted any doctor about illness for several years, an autopsy was performed on the body in Singapore before the death certificate could be issued. Without a certificate the body could not be released for burial. The company for whom Adam had worked and on whose behalf he was in Singapore sent a message asking what I wanted done about his burial. They suggested that the interment should be in Singapore where he had died but I insisted that he be brought home. Anything else was unthinkable and when the row broke out about where the men killed in the Falklands fighting should be buried, I felt deeply for the families involved. It takes much longer to recover from a death if there is no funeral ritual, no coffin to cry over or ceremony to go through. Some years ago a New Zealand plane crashed on a Polar icecap and it was decided that no attempt could be made to retrieve the bodies. Doctors were then surprised to find how much psychological disturbance there was among the people who were bereaved and teams of psychiatrists had to be called in to counsel them. They realized that those bad reactions came about because the people involved had not been able to go through the release and catharsis of a funeral.

We had to wait almost a fortnight before Adam's body could be returned to England and for me the days were passed in a sort of disbelieving suspension. Everything seemed to have stopped and it was strange to see cars driving past the house and to realize that for the rest of the world life was going on as usual. My horizons were bounded by going to bed at night fuddled with tranquillizers and waking every morning to the fresh realization of what had happened. I went out, ate meals, talked and made plans but little of that time has stayed in my memory. My son's ninth birthday party was held as planned. The invitations had been sent out before Adam died and I thought I could not disappoint young Adam. Moreover the idea of ringing round the invitees to say 'The party is cancelled because my husband died on Sunday' was more than I could bear. Ten small boys were delivered to our house that afternoon by parents who were unaware of what had happened to us. The guests tore round the house, fought and stuffed themselves with food while I watched them like a woman in a trance.

Two incidents stand out from those shrouded days.

An old man who always wore a black beret and huge boots swept the street in front of our house every day. He took excessive care with his work and even turned out on Sundays and holidays with his barrow and brush. Untidiness so offended him that he would stop and come into our front gardens to pick discarded sweet papers off the rose bushes. In an otherwise unfriendly street he was the one person I wanted to tell about Adam's death so one morning I rushed down the stairs to catch him on his rounds. We had only lived there for eighteen months and must have been strangers to him but he listened gravely, leaning on his brush, while I spoke. When I had finished he shook his head and said, 'It's very sad. I'm very sorry.'

For the same unexplained reason I suddenly said to the old couple in the off-licence, 'My husband died last week.' I was in the process of buying a bottle of whisky and the words dropped out of me in the same way as I would make an observation about the weather. As soon as I said them, it seemed totally bizarre and the couple looked at each other in horror.

The company had said they would pay for the funeral and Adam's friend Peter took the burden of making the arrangements off my shoulders. One day he rang to tell me that the body was arriving by plane from Singapore that afternoon and we ought to go that evening to the undertaker's office to make the final arrangements for the funeral. All day I thought about the body of my husband coming back to London. In imagination I travelled with it in the hold of the plane, down in the hydraulic ramp that unloaded the hold and into some enormous shed where it would lie till the undertaker called to collect it.

That evening Peter parked his car in the grounds of Brompton Oratory and we walked across the road to the undertaker's parlour – what a horrible word. I had never been in such a place before and was chilled by the semi-sanctified atmosphere, by the way all communications were made in hushed tones as if not to disturb the dead sleeping somewhere in the back premises.

A young man in a dark business suit came into the room where Peter and I were sitting and we started to talk. I wanted a funeral service in a church followed by cremation. The ashes would then be taken to Scotland and interred in Adam's family grave in the churchyard of St Michael's in Musselburgh where we had been married. The undertaker said all this was possible and then suddenly produced two small boxes made of metal. For a moment I did not realize what they were. He offered me a choice – 'Do you prefer bronze or copper?' I stared at them, laughter rising inside my throat. Could one of those boxes contain all that was to be left of a man? Could Adam whom I had loved, who had been my husband and the father of my children be consigned for eternity into a casket of bronze or copper? I began to chatter uncontrollably.

'Does it really matter? It's just like choosing a hat.'

Peter was a Roman Catholic and he thought that I ought to view Adam's body. However, when he heard that I was going to the funeral parlour my doctor had given me some advice.

'Whatever you do, don't let anyone force you into looking at the body. Try to remember him as you last saw him. If you look at his body you will only remember him as a corpse.'

So in spite of well-meant blandishments I said that I did not want to see my husband. Peter disapproved of this dereliction on my part and said that he would go into the room next door and pay his last respects to his friend. When he came back he was wiping his eyes and, sitting down heavily beside me, said, 'It's him all right.'

That made me realize that, like me, Peter had trouble believing that the vital, irrepressible Adam was actually dead. It also laid to rest my own lingering doubts about the identity of the dead man.

'Please go in,' he said to me. 'It's your duty.'

I entered the little room and sat in a straight-backed chair drawn up beside a huge coffin of yellow, highly polished wood. It looked enormous – was he really as big as that? I noticed that it was incongruously decorated on each corner with ornate roses made of brass.

'You would hate those roses, they are not your style at all,' I said to the man inside the yellow wood. After the cremation I remember someone giving me one of those terrible roses and on the way home in the funeral car I took it out of my handbag and threw it from the window somewhere in the middle of the Old Kent Road.

The coffin lid was loose. 'Just lift one corner and take a look,' said the undertaker, who also seemed to think that I ought to view the body. I sat there looking at the untightened screws but not daring to put my hand on them. If the lid had lifted of its own volition I would not have been surprised, but I was incapable of lifting it myself, I was so afraid. Half of me scolded, 'You must, you must!' but I feared that what I would see might drive me raving mad like a character in a Gothic novel. I put my head between my hands and tried to pray but all I could think was 'It's not as if I don't love you. It is just that I couldn't stand seeing you dead.'

I cannot make up my mind whether I was right or wrong. Would I have been able to come to terms with the finality of his death more quickly if I had seen his body? Today when I remember my husband I see him as he was during the first few years of our marriage when we were blissfully happy together. We lived then in a house outside Bombay. It was called the Gulmohurs and had huge, red-flowered trees growing in the garden. I see him there, beneath the glorious trees, wearing faded blue shorts and laughing. Would I have that memory if I had seen him dead?

In a moment of confidence I told Adam's sister about my inability to look at him and she was disappointed and disapproving. 'If it had been me, I would have looked at him,' she said. Perhaps she is a stronger woman than me, perhaps she is a more feeling one, but to this day I still cannot pass that corner of Brompton Road where the undertaker's office stood without a shiver of apprehension.

Before my own close experience of death, I would have agreed with the cynic who said, 'Funerals have more regard for the vanity of the living than the honour of the dead.' The house we lived in was at the side of the A2 and processions of funeral cars often passed the kitchen window on their way to nearby cemeteries. Sometimes the coffins were piled high with flowers and the carrying racks on the roofs of the hearses were domed with multi-coloured wreaths. Some of the offerings were vast and must have been very expensive – cushions of carnations with 'Goodbye Dad' on them, red and white hearts, once an enormous motor cycle made of flowers. When I was deep in grief however those tributes no longer seemed vulgar or excessive and if I had been able to find a florist to sell me a cushion with Adam's name on it, I think I would have bought it. I yearned to send him off with some outrageous gesture.

Funerals fulfil a very useful function for the bereaved because the ceremony is used to mark the transcendental moment when the finality of death is realized – it satisfies a deep and primitive need in us all. One widow told me that the funeral of her husband was 'a joyous occasion . . . We opened the roof of the crematorium and the sun poured down on his coffin. Afterwards we went home and held a party. His family were deeply shocked but I felt that we were celebrating the end of his life in the way he would have wanted.'

Another widow with a deep religious belief said her husband's funeral was 'glorious', in spite of her deep grief.

'I could almost hear the trumpets sounding on the other side,' she said, 'and I was greatly comforted during the months that followed by my ecstatic feelings that day.'

A widower who had every reason to be reconciled to the death of his wife because she had suffered from a disabling and ultimately crippling disease said:

'When she died I knew it was a release for me as well as for her. I could have spent the rest of my life pushing her around in a wheelchair. In spite of that I felt a climacteric of grief at her funeral, a spilling out of feeling that had been pent up for so long. The funeral was a shattering experience but once it was over I felt truly free.'

Two women who had been mistresses of men who died unexpectedly also talked about how they felt on their lovers' funeral days. Both men were married so the mistresses had no acknowledged right to grief or official place in the funeral ritual. The first woman did not even attend the ceremony because although she was known slightly by the wife and family there was no ostensible reason why she should attend. His death only came to her knowledge through an entry in the 'Deaths' column of their local newspaper.

'The afternoon he was being buried, I could not go to work. Instead I lay in bed with the alarm clock beside me, fixed to go off at three o'clock when I knew the ceremony was to take place. As soon as it rang I began to weep. It was the only time I gave way to my grief but I cried so much I thought I was going to die. Next day I had to go back to work and there was no one with whom I could discuss my feelings. The funeral – even though I was not there – gave me a focus for mourning.'

The second woman had lived with a man intermittently for eight years and their association was known to the wife and their mutual friends. She said:

'I went to his funeral but I felt it was best for me to keep a low profile so I stood at the back and tried not to break down too obviously. Some people who realized what it was like for me came up and patted me on the back. After all you don't go through eight years with a man and not suffer hell when he dies. Most of the sympathy was directed at his widow however who was weeping and carrying on, having to be supported at the grave and that sort of thing. I knew how bad their relationship had really been and I knew too that I was, the one who had loved him best but I could not show my feelings. In spite of that, going to his funeral helped me a lot.'

It did not seem possible that I would be able to get through Adam's funeral without collapsing. The ceremony was held in the church in Central London where our daughter Eleanor had been christened little more than a year previously. The minister, Dr Fraser McCluskey, was very kind to me, visited us and helped us pick the hymns for the service. We chose Adam's favourites and I could hear him in memory singing them – 'Onward Christian Soldiers' and 'To Be a Pilgrim'. For several years after the funeral the minister continued to visit the children and I and we greatly appreciated this, especially after most other sympathizers had long ago disappeared and we felt as if the outside world had forgotten all about us.

On the morning of the funeral I woke up feeling battered and only with difficulty succeeded in dressing myself in the funeral clothes. Before being a widow myself I would have disdained the idea of going into black to signify mourning but when it actually happened nothing else seemed suitable. I already owned a black coat and somewhere in the depths of my wardrobe was a box with a black hat. I searched them out now not purely for reasons of economy but because the idea of going out to shop for anything new was more than I could contemplate. As I sat on the bed waiting for the funeral cars to arrive, I spoke to Adam's deity:

'If you get me through this I will never worry about anything else again.'

A crowd of people, family and friends, stood awkwardly around in the hall and I moved about amongst them feeling as if I was in some way set apart. In the first car with me was my mother, the three eldest children and Lorna, my friend. The route went through the seedy streets of Catford and Lewisham and while we drove along my mother chattered incessantly in an effort to divert my mind. Listening I felt blind rage rising until I shouted out, 'For God's sake just keep quiet.' I had never spoken to her in that way before. For the rest of the trip we all sat in silence. As the car drew up in front of the church I saw some friends on the pavement and half raised my hand to wave to them because for a few seconds I did not remember why they were there.

My plea was answered because miraculously I did get through the funeral with a certain degree of composure although I failed to keep my promise about never worrying again. The funeral address which I had asked a friend to deliver introduced a note of controversy into the proceedings because our friend was a humanist and he said that no matter what we felt about an afterlife, it was only necessary to give thanks for the man as we had known him. It was not necessary to console ourselves with the idea that Adam had gone on to some higher place. Those sentiments coincided with my own but not, of course, with those of the clergyman who stood up beneath the pulpit and, throwing back his leonine white head, roared in glorious affirmation: 'Man's soul is immortal.' This delighted me because I knew how much Adam would have relished theological debate breaking out over his body.

The church was full for over two hundred people had come from all over the country and I was grateful to them all for showing their appreciation by attending. When the ceremony was over I adopted the old Scottish custom of standing at the door of the church with my children and shaking hands with everyone as they came out – that way I was able to see and thank them all. Only a few people came with me to the crematorium and then afterwards to a funeral tea in a Kensington hotel. There the atmosphere was like a party with people meeting again after many years but though I spoke to many people and in a way almost enjoyed the experience, only part of me was there.

Adam's burying was a painful and protracted affair because of my own insistence that his ashes should be taken to Scotland. By the time of the second ceremony a couple of weeks later, all impetus had left me and instead of exaltation I only felt a deadening grief and a terrible weariness. The interment of the ashes was attended by those of Adam's friends who had not been able to go to London and we stood round the open grave in flurries of snow while an unknown minister in a top hat said a few words over the bronze casket. It was buried with only a small bunch of snowdrops on top of it.

That ceremony made me aware how practical we were being about disposing of a man's human remains; as Tennessee Williams said, 'When a man burns, he leaves only a handful of ashes.' The desolation that came to me with that thought has made it impossible for me to have any emotional link with that grave for I am sure that nothing of Adam lies there and I never visit it.

The children did not go with me to the second funeral because I felt that one burying was harrowing enough for them. My mother-in-law was ill in bed, confused in her mind about what had happened and we did not then anticipate that the family would be regathered round the same graveside only a month later for her burial. That time of my life seems like an unrelenting period of mourning and funerals.

After the short ceremony I was given a double whisky which I drank without realizing the influence it could have on my tranquillized body. I was alone that day, driving the company car which had been part of Adam's salary and which I had been told could either be purchased by me at market price or returned to the company as soon as the Scottish funeral was over. When I was driving away from a set of traffic lights, I swerved and scraped the side of the car next to me. The driver was understandably furious and jumped out shaking his fist at me through the glass of my window but what he saw sitting there must have shocked him because he suddenly went quiet. I rolled down the window and said: 'I'm sorry. It was my fault but I've just buried my husband. Here is the address of the company that owns this car. Put your claim in to them.'

One of Adam's business cards was lying on the dashboard and I handed it over with no remorse for passing my problems on to the company who were rapidly becoming the major hate object in my life.

Next day was Christmas Eve and we spent it in a cottage in the Scottish Borders which Adam had bought two weeks before he died. That night I was crawling over the floor, tacking down a carpet and the children were putting tinsel which we had bought from the village shop on a small fir tree when there was a knock at the door. On the step was a lady from the village who we had never met but who had heard about what had happened. She said quite simply:

'I heard about your husband and I have just come along to say how sorry I am.'

We welcomed her in and sat drinking tea together. I don't think she could possibly have known what an act of kindness that visit was to us. Next day it was Christmas and no words can describe the desolation of my feelings. Even thinking about what had happened brought a physical pain to my heart and I remember making custard sauce with tears running down into the mixing bowl. Soon afterwards we returned to London and there was nothing to look forward to – the rest of my life lay ahead of me, bleak and lonely without Adam.

# 3

## *Sympathy but not Pity*

ANYONE who can bear grief alone must be of titanic strength. The first essential in bereavement is sympathy, the giving and receiving of which is not easy – often it is one of the most difficult things to learn.

The person who is sympathized with is often resentful: 'Don't pity me' is their reaction. I hated the idea of being an object of pity but in spite of that I very much needed sympathy.

The dictionary makes clear the distinction between the two words – to 'pity' means to commiserate with or to be sorry for but 'in modern use', says my dictionary, 'it implies slight contempt for a person on account of some moral or intellectual inferiority.' 'Sympathy' is very different and it is defined as 'a feeling of compassion or commiseration, a quality of thus being affected by the sufferings of others'. People who sympathize weep with you, those who pity can manage to convey the feeling that what has happened has in some way lowered you in their eyes or that, and this is worst of all, 'you had it coming to you', as the song says. Sympathizers must know when to stop because over-protection can prevent the bereaved making any effort to recover themselves. Pitiers on the other hand can often have a spine-stiffening function because they can so antagonize the person they are pitying that they force them back on to their own feet.

It is sad when someone who is mourning becomes so muddled in their feelings that they confuse sympathy with pity. There is a time in suffering when sympathy is all important but later those who have been sympathized with reach the stage of wanting to break away from those who have helped them.

Elizabeth Bowen, the novelist, wrote in *The Death of the Heart*: 'There is no consoler, no confidant that half of the instinct does not want to reject. The spilling over, the bursting out of tears and words, the ejaculation of private grief accomplishes itself like a convulsion in circumstances that no one would ever choose.'

It is indeed difficult not to feel shame when you meet people who saw you in your weeping agony, especially if they did not weep with you. Ten years after my own widowing, I still feel embarrassment when I remember some of the things I said in front of friends and when I meet them I wonder awkwardly if they remember too.

A wise friend who has taken the trouble to console and help many widowed men and women has helped me very much in writing this book. She said that one of the things about the role of sympathizer that has saddened her is the knowledge that she will often end up by being rejected – this is most particularly the case with men who seem to resent having showed their weaker side to an outsider. She and her husband have several times helped widowers who ended up by cutting themselves off completely especially if they remarried. One man with whom they were very friendly went to Australia and remarried without even telling the family of his first wife to whom he had been extremely devoted during his wife's lifetime.

'Now I see that this is in fact a very normal way to behave,' said my friend, 'and perhaps it is a compliment in a way because it shows that whatever help we have been able to give has been constructive and people reach a point where they are strong enough to be independent and discard the people who were around when they felt most lost. If I have any criticism of this attitude, I would say that once they are back on their feet it would be tactful if they considered the effect complete rejection might have on the people who helped them.'

Everyone needs help at first. I was amazed to read in *A Book of Etiquette* by Lady Troubridge, published in 1929 and reprinted in the late 1950s, that the widowed should not be visited at all except by close relatives for at least a month and for two months they should not make visits themselves. If anyone did call within the forbidden weeks, the widow or widower should not meet them because they might be in danger of breaking down and giving way to 'unseemly emotion'. It is remarkable how much popular understanding of the needs of the mourning has changed because now it is recognized how valuable it is for sympathizers just to sit and listen, to allow the bereaved to talk about their grief and to weep if necessary. The old-fashioned wake, which Lady Troubridge would probably have disdained, is a primitive expression of this need.

The bereaved need people, they need continual support in the beginning, a constant repetition of the same words. In the days after Adam's death I had a certain satisfaction about repeating over and over again the few facts I knew of his death, like retelling something I had read in a novel. If I had not told the story so often in an almost unending monologue I doubt if I would be able to believe it, even now.

The expressions of concern that I valued most were not the bunches of flowers or the potted plants which kind people did send, but physical expressions of concern – the hug, the kiss on the cheek, the hand on the arm. Physical contact is one of the most reassuring manifestations of real concern because it is very difficult for people to reach out and touch people they do not like. Widowed people who are starved of physical contact often say that they are more conscious of the need to reach out and touch others than they were when they were married. Touching is a kind of reassurance. It can, however, be misunderstood and once at a dinner party I innocently put my hand on the arm of the young man sitting next to me who had said something which made me feel in contact with him. Over the table I suddenly saw his wife stiffen and it taught me that widows should always think before yielding to the temptation to touch. Newspaper advertisements for companions often refer to the yearning for physical contact, particularly the longing for someone to hold hands with; a young widower recently advertised for a lady who like him had noticed 'handholding couples in the park'.

Many people are reluctant to intrude on grief because they are afraid that they will be 'in the way'. But they are wrong. Sympathy need not be vastly time consuming – all that is needed is a word on the telephone, a note through the post. Anyone who is prepared to go farther can make a visit or extend a genuine offer of help. Even if people who come to sympathize are 'looking for particulars', that does not detract from the value of their sympathy at the time. I still feel resentment about one old friend who did not get in touch after

Adam died. We heard nothing of her for a couple of years until a letter arrived out of the blue explaining that she had felt inadequate to say the right things at the time. Only in the last paragraph of her letter did I come upon what seemed to be the real reason for her writing. She had heard a broadcast I had done on 'Woman's Hour' and had often wanted to write something for the programme . . . could I advise her how to get started or even better introduce her to the editor? Her letter ended up in the wastepaper basket and was never answered.

Friends who failed me, however, were few and in the days after Adam died the phone kept ringing. I always rushed to answer it myself because I wanted to talk about what had happened and in a strange way I was still subconsciously hoping that it would be his voice at the other end of the line and the bubble of horror that was encasing me would be broken. But the voices always asked the same question.

'I've just heard the most awful rumour about your Adam. Surely it isn't true?'

I was grateful to people who took the trouble to call and to those who offered us help. My neighbour was a perfect example of this because without being asked she took upon herself the task of buying our food for the first weeks after Adam's death. She remembered even to buy cat and dog food though she kept no pets herself. I remember her staggering into the kitchen under the weight of huge cardboard boxes packed high with provisions. Other people took the children out to the cinema or to the park and invitations came for me to go out for drinks or for dinner. Practical offers of help are what is most needed, however, and, once made, those offers should always be followed up. It is not sufficient to say airily, 'Just give me a ring if you need anything,' or 'Let me know if the children would like an outing.' Invitations and offers should be specific and not made as some sort of empty gesture because the person who receives them will be reluctant to lift the phone and ask for help. Only once did I ask a friend to give me a lift into London because I had an appointment there soon after Adam died. She forgot all about it when the time came. In ordinary times this would have been dismissed as a mild inconvenience or even funny but in my ultra-sensitive state it seemed the most terrible let down – I had asked for help and she had not even thought it sufficiently important to remember. The experience of receiving help and sympathy has taught me how remiss I have been in the past myself towards anyone in need of consolation.

Very many people of my acquaintance felt that it would do me good to get out of the house for an evening but in time I grew to dread some of those invitations, especially the ones that were phrased, 'Pop along for supper. It's just me and my husband.' I felt as if I was being fitted in, fobbed off, they were doing their duty by me. Those evenings were agony, sitting around in an awkward threesome watching the clock out of the corner of my eye until the time came to make my escape. Often the host couple use anyone who is single or a widow as a sort of catalyst against whom to bounce their own disagreements. When you are out of the game the state of play can be shown more honestly to you. By refusing those evenings of marital wrangling however my social isolation grew worse because the people who invite you to supper for three never think to include you in more convivial gatherings – those are all for safely paired-off couples.

It would, of course, be wrong to infer that all our friends were found wanting. I could not have survived the first period of widowhood without the help and sympathy which was so freely extended to me. I remember one man who had been a friend of my husband and who sent me a message after the funeral to say that if I needed money he would give – not lend – me £2000. The vastness of this offer totally staggered me and I was touched and surprised by his generosity. Though I did not need or take the money I knew the offer was sincerely meant.

Practical help also came from another old friend who was herself a widow but who I had not seen for several years. She telephoned and asked if she could visit me and when she turned up the sight of her was infinitely reassuring because she showed that life does indeed go on after widowhood. She was full of wise, realistic advice and did not attempt to minimize what I was feeling and would continue to feel for some time.

'Don't expect to forget what has happened, you never will but the pain does die down in time. You have had a good marriage and if you are going to avoid loneliness, you must find something else to fill your life. My advice is get a job and concentrate on making a future for yourself and your children. Don't concentrate too much of yourself on them either because they are going to grow up and leave you. You must make your own life now.'

Her advice proved to be most valuable and I repeat it for other widows secure in the knowledge that it helped me.

But the biggest piece of practical help came from Adam's previous employer who rang up when he heard about his death simply to ask, 'Are you all right?'

I said I didn't know because I was so confused.

'I mean how are you off for money?'

Until than I had not given the problem of money a thought.

'What is his company doing for you?'

I had heard nothing from them.

'You need a lawyer,' said the old employer. 'Do you have one?'

I had no lawyer. In fact Adam did not even leave a will. When he heard that our friend just said, 'Don't worry, I'll find you someone.'

He arranged for his company lawyer to shoulder the extra burden of me and my family and for five years until we left London he handled without charge our affairs which were very complex because of Adam's intestacy.

The lawyer's help, and the calm reassurance which he was able to give me through periods when I was almost distracted with worry and inability to cope, made it possible for me to survive sufficiently unscarred to be writing this book today.

The helpful friends I have described so far were all sympathizers who proved to be helpful. Condolences that could well be done without came from doleful Jeremiahs – usually women – who gave forth utterances like 'Things will be worse before they are better,' and 'It will be at least five years before you feel yourself again.' Someone actually said that to me at a time when five years felt like an eternity. They all meant well but if I had listened to them suicide would have seemed a preferable alternative to the continuing glooms of widowhood. The sister of a woman recently widowed said to me:

'I just wish that half of the women who go to see my sister would stay away. They say such depressing things to her that when they leave she is more forlorn than she was before they arrived.'

Awkward sympathizers do not help much either because they flounder around not knowing what to say and proffer phrases like . . . 'Of course he didn't suffer,' and 'You're lucky to have the children.' If the widowed person has no children they are just as likely to be told they are lucky to have no one depending on them. I was told 'You're lucky enough to be so young that someone else can come along' and 'Adam would have made a terrible invalid.' I knew all those things but in no way did they reconcile me to his death.

The people who lived through the wall in our pair of semi-detached houses were a family with young children. When we moved in the wife pointedly said that our predecessors had been the perfect neighbours – 'We never saw them.' Communication between us was perfunctory and Adam was buried before the neighbours even realized he was dead.

I wondered how they managed to avoid seeing the cortege which had moved away from our shared frontage. One day however my neighbour and I met on the pavement and she said, 'I've just heard about your husband, I'm very sorry.' If she had left it at that, I would have been satisfied but on she went: 'I suppose it's like the break-up of a love affair really, things get better after a while.'

Suddenly I saw her with new eyes, a tall, elegant girl who was pitifully unaware of what love meant. She had not the slightest idea of what it was like to lose another person who was literally half of yourself.

The feelings of anger and annoyance I felt at misdirected sympathy are shared by many widowed people. A widower, who in all other respects was the soul of reason, told how he felt that every nerve was ultra-sensitive and liable to spark off into resentment after his wife's death.

'People who sympathized with me were especially very trying. I began to feel that it ought to be me who was consoling them. It became so distressing that I used to cross the street if

I saw anyone coming who I knew would want to speak to me about it.'

A widow also felt that sympathizers all 'said the wrong thing'. She recalled, 'I went back to work two days after my husband died and I did not refer to it at all. My children were grown up and they were a great help because we were able to talk it all out together and I felt we had said all there was to say. People outside the family only seemed to say stupid things.'

Strangely, clichéd statements that would grate on me if they were spoken did not offend nearly so much when they were written in letters. In fact they seemed to comfort me. Every morning I rushed downstairs to collect the letters off the mat and read them over and over again, treasuring each one as a tangible proof that Adam had been esteemed by people outside his own family. In a way I needed those letters as proof that he had existed outside my imagination – a sort of Bishop Berkeley's theory in reverse. Finally I collected all the letters into a box file and have kept them for our descendants.

The most affecting letter in the file came from Babu, our Indian bearer. News of Adam's death must have reached him very quickly because the letter was one of the first to arrive, carefully written in a schoolboyish hand on flimsy blue paper. Babu's English was rudimentary and he could not write so I knew that he had gone to one of the letter writers who set up their booths alongside Bombay's railway stations to write letters for those who are illiterate. As I read Babu's letter I could hear his voice dictating what he wanted to say to the letter writer.

'I was very very sorry to hear the sad news of sab. I was so shocked I did not know what to do. I am always remembering you and sab and thinking of the children. I will always pray that God will keep you. Please do not worry, it is all God's wish.'

As I said when discussing the difference between pity and sympathy – those who come to pity often fulfil a very useful function. Resentment can be a dynamic force for it steels the will and gives a determination to battle through even if it is only to prove the pitiers wrong.

The woman who called on me one afternoon could have had little idea of the function she was fulfilling as she looked round the sitting-room and said in a voice that barely hid her satisfaction: 'I don't suppose you will be able to keep all this on. It's far too big. You'll have to sell it and buy one of those little places up on the estate.'

I knew that one of the little places on the estate did not appeal either to her or to me but she was relegating me to my new life . . . 'What a pity about poor Liz, she used to have such a nice house.' Inwardly I promised myself that I would not sell the house, I would show her I was capable of carrying the burden of it alone.

My determination to do so was increased when the appraiser came to estimate the value of the house for estate duty. In those days the duty had to be paid by widows on the family home – that has since been abolished fortunately for widows now. In the past it brought dreadful problems if a woman was widowed with a house but no money because she had to find the cash to pay the estate duty if she wanted to go on living in her home. Our house had risen dramatically in value since we bought it only eighteen months before and I was very worried about how I was going to pay the duty. The assessor looked round in congratulation which I could have well done without – 'It's a nice house,' he said. 'What a pity you'll have to leave but I suppose a little bungalow in Surrey is what you will want now.'

A house up on the estate or a bungalow in Surrey – those were the choices open to me as far as the pitiers were concerned. I could not see why the disappearance of one person from a family of six automatically meant that all the others' lives were radically changed. I was now expected to do penance for my previous affluence by spending the rest of my years in a trim and economical home, keeping a low profile. I was determined not to accept this for I was only forty and still had unfulfilled ambitions and hopes. I had to prove to the outside world that I was not so worthless that when my husband died I slipped away into obscurity – if I had done, I reasoned, he would not have been justified in marrying me in the first place so I owed it to him to try to keep our lifestyle going in as near the old way as possible.

Today more women are realizing their own claims to an individual destiny that is not necessarily linked to that of their protector-man. Now that younger women go out to work after marriage as a matter of course and share the family income and responsibility with their men, the next crop of widows should be able to face life on their own with much less trauma.

# 4

## The Time of Desolation

FROM time to time photographs of grieving widows appear in the newspapers and I always find them heart rending because I can see in the stricken faces so many of the feelings that I experienced myself. A recent one particularly moved me – a front page picture in the *Sunday Times* of a young Falkland Islands widow, sitting alone, surrounded by the letters and postcards which had been sent to her by her dead husband. Her attitude, head bent over a crumpled letter, summed up so much that I remember of the terrible desolation that comes when the full realization of what has happened begins to sink in, when the solicitude of friends begins to wear thin and life is a bleak vista of unending misery.

This is the time when depression rules your life. F. Scott Fitzgerald, a man who had his share of desolation and despair, succinctly summed it up as 'always three o'clock in the morning'. It was the nadir of my life. Never had I been so desperate and I hope never to feel that way again. I do not think I could survive it twice and I sympathize with a widow who told me she had no wish to remarry in case she had to experience another widowing.

In the normal course of events, three months are given for someone to 'return to normal': after that, invitations drop off, callers disappear, the rest of the world goes swinging on and the widowed are expected to pick up what is left of their lives and make the best of it. 'Making a good recovery', 'getting better every day', 'coping so well' are some of the things people say about acceptable cases; 'not snapping out of it', 'a little self-indulgent' dismisses the others. People who care about someone who has been widowed should perhaps continue to cosset them for a little longer than they do at present because there is no time limit on how long sorrow lasts and each case takes its own time.

I once went to a party and met a woman who turned on me with venom.

'I hated you,' she said. 'When my husband was killed people who knew you kept telling me how well you had managed. I just hated the sound of you.'

I wanted very much to tell her how my 'coping very well' attitude had been sheer playacting and bravado. Underneath I was a quaking morass of nerves and insecurities. But unfortunately people outside only see what they choose to see and often do not look any deeper.

I suppose that my besetting sin is pride and it has made me always try to present a good front to the world. 'If you do not esteem yourself, no one else will esteem you,' has been my lifelong guideline and I have tried to live up to it even though much of the self-esteem which I present to the outside is really a defensive wall. Widows can be excused for taking a very bad fall in their self-esteem during the first period of widowing. As they are left more and more to their own devices, they become convinced that the society of which they used to be a part only tolerated them because of their husbands. Without him there no longer seems to be any place for them. Suddenly all the friends they had seem to have been his friends and if the social circle in which a couple moved was based around his interests the situation is particularly difficult. Inevitably, the widow is dropped and she finds that she has no circle of her own to settle back into. Hostesses are not prepared to make a seat at their tables for a single woman. At a concert not long ago, I heard a woman in front of me call across to another couple, 'Come to dinner on Saturday; I'm having Henry – he's the odd, interesting man.'

Who would ever invite a couple to meet the 'odd, interesting woman' even if she was twice as nice and three times as intelligent as Henry? What gives Henry his seat at the dinner table is the fact that he was born a man. If only society was not so strictly divided into the couple and the single man set against the 'all-women' affairs. Once I invited a couple to dinner to meet a female friend who I thought would interest them. The wife turned my invitation down flat – 'My husband hates those all-women affairs,' she said. If my other guest had been a dull man instead of an interesting woman they would have come without demur.

The well-meant efforts of organizations like Cruse which try to reintegrate the widow into society are frequently offering only a society as lost and searching as the person to be relocated. They are a collection of outcasts from the world of the couples. A recent widow told me about her feelings when she went to her first Cruse meeting:

'We all gathered together one afternoon and sat around with our children at our feet making bright conversation. The woman who was the organizer was trying very hard to "cheer us all up" – making bright chat about where she and her husband had gone for their summer holidays. I could think of no subject that was less appropriate and the talk only intensified my misery. I could see it was not doing much for the rest of the widows either. I sat there and thought to myself "What am I doing here? Is this what the rest of my life is to be like?" I left and I have never gone back.'

Her main complaint against Cruse was that most of the volunteer helpers who she met were not themselves widows. Questioned about this a Cruse organizer said that it was not necessary to have been widowed to appreciate the problems of those who were and at times it was actually better to be able to view the problems from a dispassionate viewpoint. I find it hard to agree on that point because although my own imagination has always been pretty active, it would have been impossible for me to imagine the depth of misery that can engulf the newly widowed or take account of the many strands of emotional conflict with which they have to cope. Widows do not want dispassionate advice for they can get plenty of that from their family and friends. When they go to an organization like Cruse, they want to be able to unburden themselves to someone who will understand what they are saying and not criticize them for feeling as they do. They want to discuss honestly with other people their frailties, agonies and resentments, real or imagined. And above all they want to be treated again as a 'normal' person, not as some sort of social misfit. They want to be reintegrated into the world they have always known but perhaps that is too much to ask in a world where hostesses still think of table settings as man/woman, man/woman – 'and if you have any physical attraction left you might as well give up,' said one angry widow, 'because it is always the women who do the inviting.'

Another suggestion for easing the pain of widowhood ante-dates the death of a partner and is related to the inability of the present day to acknowledge the inevitability of death. Anyone who is in love and who values their partner above all others must not allow that love to blind them to the possibility of loss. Somerset Maugham was talking about his homosexual lover when he wrote – 'The tragedy of true love is that one must die before the other' – and that tragedy applies to all kinds of love. It would enhance the happiness people feel in each other if they were always aware of the transience of life. It is not morbid to arm yourself in advance against the possibility of being left alone and your love and esteem for someone else would be heightened by the occasional thought of what life would be like without them. It would certainly make people more aware of happiness when they had it and put a new perspective on the antagonisms and difficulties that can arise between two people no matter how much they love each other.

Among the people I have talked to about this book, the old adjusted best to widowhood. This contradicts the findings of the social researchers who thought that the old were most seriously affected – 'It's the next big area of concern,' said one enthusiastic young woman. Another social worker explained her findings about the old by saying:

'Often they appear to pick up the threads of their lives by going out to play bridge or golf and visiting their children and grandchildren but in fact their lives are never the same again.'

She overlooked the undeniable fact that no one who is widowed can ever expect life to be the same again and only a few are ever lucky enough to achieve another kind of happiness. Younger people put on a brave front of acceptance which allows the rest of society comfortably to overlook them. They do not probe too deeply in case what they find appals them. I found that those people who were widowed later in life – if they were reasonable, thinking people – have a kind of metaphysical acceptance about the death of a partner. They are still sad but it is something they have thought about. A poem by Robert Burns sums up the serenity and acceptance that can come with age. His words are put into the mouth of a woman looking lovingly at her white-haired husband and musing on the transience of both their lives. The poem is called 'John Anderson, My Jo'– the word 'Jo' means sweetheart.

> John Anderson, my jo, John,
> When we were first acquent,
> Your locks were like the raven,
> Your bonny brow was brent.
> But now we're growing old, John,
> Your locks are like the snow.
> But blessings on your frosty pow,
> John Anderson, my jo.

That is not a sentimental poem. It is a moving acknowledgement that 'one must die before the other'.

I was as guilty as any blind mole of closing my eyes to mortality and was less armoured than many women against the possibility of my husband dying. He was young and very fit; he had never been ill through the years we were married. Six months before his death he had passed a medical examination that was needed for our mortgage. 'Just cut down on your smoking' was the only advice the doctor gave to him. Adam smoked about sixty cigarettes a day and though from time to time he attempted to cut back, he never succeeded for more than a few days. I was however convinced that, if not actually immortal, he would certainly live on to his nineties and I would be the first to die.

Like all lovers we from time to time indulged in sentimental talk about what would happen if one of us was to die, but to me the thought of his death was purely academic. The idea that he would in time be left a widower caused me a certain amount of wistful unhappiness and I would indulge myself with wondering whether he would marry again. What would his second wife be like? Would she be someone we already knew? I worried about what would happen to my children under those circumstances and I remember now the time I wasted on my pointless speculations.

Looking back now I can see that until the day I became a widow I led a charmed life, bastioned by the sure knowledge that no matter what problem cropped up, there was someone beside me to help me cope with it. It seemed as if I lived inside a suit of magic armour. As a child I had complete trust in my father and when I married I passed that reliance on to my husband, so much so that Adam seemed super powerful in my eyes. I greatly admired his capacity to cut through crises, to make decisions, to sort everything out. My dependence on him was carried to a point of superstition and if I had to tackle anything I deeply dreaded, it was essential that he accompany me; I even made him go with me to the dentist. I loathe flying but could go on long air trips if he was beside me – no plane, I was sure, would be so inconsiderate as to crash with him aboard.

When our son was three he became ill with an undiagnosed complaint and caused us great anxiety because there was some suspicion that it was heart trouble. I always insisted that Adam phoned up for the results of the various tests they did on young Adam because I was sure that if it was me hanging on to the other end of the line, the prognosis would be bad. When everything turned out well and the fears proved unfounded, I was sure that it was Adam's intervention that had turned bad luck away from us. I knew that all those ideas of mine were without logical basis but he was my life's crutch and the thought of having to go on without him was literally terrifying.

When Adam was alive, from time to time I would come across an article in a newspaper or magazine about the life of the widow or the miseries of divorce. Superstitiously I turned over the pages quickly like someone averting their eyes from a portent of bad luck – 'That doesn't apply to my life,' I thought. So when widowhood did come, it burst on me like a bomb. I was totally unprepared because I had actively prevented myself from thinking it could ever happen. When I was blasted out of my safe complacency I showed every sign of wandering around shell-shocked.

Yet strangely in spite of the death certificate and the burying, the weeping and the pain, there was still inside me a childish hope mingled with disbelief – 'This can't be happening to *me*.' Some nebulous outside agency, some sort of protective magic would surely take over and make everything right again. For years I had to fight against my unrealistic belief in a fairy godmother who would take my life over and sort out the problems. A secure, protected childhood is good in many ways but it does not teach you that life is going to kick you in the teeth and there may be no one to come to your aid.

Many of the books and articles written about widowhood and grieving say that the experience passes in 'stages'. I do agree that you pass through defined reactions and in the end it is possible to end up in a new kind of happiness and with a new philosophy – you can be 'cured' – but I disagree with the simplistic labelling of each 'stage'. There are no time limits to how long each reaction should last. Some people suffering from bad grief reactions worry because a certain length of time has passed and they feel no better. Other people can work through to a period of calm and resignation only to be suddenly harrowed again by feelings of deep loss and anguish. They worry in case their recovery is regressing. The 'stage' theory ignores the undeniable fact that grief, guilt, anger, re-sentment, self-pity, envy, longing, disillusion and disbelief go hand in hand through the months and the years. One will disappear for a while but suddenly spring up again like a jack in the box. The progress of widowhood can be best compared to wandering in a maze with no map to guide you. It is only to be expected that you will find yourself up several dead ends but you must always retain the determination to turn round and start all over again. Only by wandering on will you sud-denly find yourself in 'the white clearing on the other side of sorrow' – it *is* there for everyone, no matter how deep their grief or how hard they find that to accept in the beginning. What can help in tackling the maze is to be forewarned about some of the stranger manifestations that grief can bring. The first surprise is that sorrow is a physical pain and can bring on symptoms as definite as any illness.

During the first weeks on my own, my body seemed numb, almost anaesthetized. This may in part have been due to the tranquillizers which I took in the beginning but I have never regularly had recourse to medicines and very soon I stopped taking the pills. They only muffled my reactions and did nothing to blunt the edge of sorrow. It is in fact a mistake to try to avoid grieving for it is a natural reaction and one which must be gone through. I stopped taking sleeping pills as well because I was frightened by the hungover, sick feeling they gave me for most of the day as well as plunging me into a pit of blackness at night.

The lack of physical reaction was frightening and one day I was washing my hands at the sink when I realized it was possible to run scalding water over them without hurting myself. I held my hands up in front of my face and studied them dispassionately as if they belonged to someone else. This feeling of fragmentation of your own body is deeply disturbing but not at all unusual in the early days of shock. Another widow described how she also experienced the same lack of feeling.

'A few days after my husband's funeral, I decided to tidy up the garden and when I was pushing the metal wheelbarrow down the path, I tripped and fell full length over it. I was very badly cut and bleeding, my hands and knees were lacerated and my stockings all torn but it was so strange – I didn't feel a thing. The cuts and bruises seemed as if they belonged to someone else, I could dress them as if I was a nurse and during the time they took to heal I had absolutely no feeling from them.'

Recent medical research throws some light on this phenomenon because experiments with laboratory mice have shown that in certain stressful situations they can show signs of heightened pain thresholds. It has been discovered that the body contains a natural analgesic which comes into action when an individual who is being attacked gives up or resigns itself to defeat. This was proved by experiments whereby an intruder mouse was thrust into a cage where another mouse was already in established possession. The owner mouse fought off the intruder very aggressively and it was observed that when the intruder adopted a defeated attitude, it quickly became less sensitive to pain than it would normally be. The attacking mouse's pain threshold was unchanged. People in the early days of bereavement who sink into passive misery can experience a similar insensitivity to physical pain.

What can also come is a deep-seated melancholy. Doctors working at the Medical Research Council's Neuropsychiatry Laboratory at Epsom have found that hormone levels drop rapidly in people who are bereaved. This hormone drop leads to depression, but it is always essential for the depressed widow or widower to realize that what is happening to them is a purely physical reaction, that in time their hormone level will begin to rise again and the depression will slowly lift. The Epsom-based doctors have devised a test called the dexamethadone suppression test which can show them whether depression is due to a lowered hormonal level or to other, less specific causes. They can use drugs to balance the hormone level if the condition is prolonged.

Depression that goes on for a long time and seems to rule your life is called 'endogenous', meaning 'growing from within'. It can lead to mental illness if the sufferer is not reassured or if steps are not taken to counteract it. The knowledge that such depression is normal, that it has a physical cause and that time and healing will take it away can help to counteract some of the most frightening aspects of the situation of the newly widowed.

Even as recently as the nineteenth century doctors would still issue medical certificates with 'died of grief' given as the official cause of death. They knew that a broken heart can be as dangerous as any other illness. Today people still die of broken hearts but such deaths are filed under other specific causes or are looked on as a kind of weakness, a giving in. Statistics for death among newly widowed people do however pinpoint how dangerous a time it can be especially for those in the higher age groups. From time to time a death is a planned and conscious suicide – and there have been many cases of those – but other deaths are less voluntary, a kind of psychic giving up which evidences itself in a specific disease like cancer, heart trouble, ulcers, nervous breakdowns and even arthritis. 'People just give up and let a disease take them over,' said a doctor.

Statisticians have worked out a danger graph which awards points to every kind of fraught situation that can be encountered in life from moving house or being made redundant to losing a spouse which is regarded as the most dangerous of all and is awarded the highest number of points – 100. If stress is piled upon stress, the danger count becomes unendurable and illness of some sort will inevitably follow – people have heart attacks, or they can injure themselves in accidents. The number of bereaved people who break limbs or crash their cars is statistically high. The stress graphs and point systems were devised some ten years ago by a team of American researchers working with the crew of an American aircraft carrier that was out at sea for long periods of time. Because of the exclusivity of the sample, doubts have recently been thrown on the authenticity of the findings but the general principle that people suffering from bereavement are in higher danger than normal of falling ill or having an accident does seem to hold good.

Even when people do not actually become ill, they can imagine that they have done so and it is common for the bereaved to exhibit specific symptoms of the disease that killed a husband or wife. They often go to their doctors firmly convinced that they too are about to die from the disease that so recently harrowed the family. Sometimes this fear has been known to drive people to suicide when they have not actually been ill.

A doctor working in a hospice for the dying said that he always tried to point out the possibility of sympathetic illness to the family of any of his patients.

'If people are aware that they can suddenly develop the same symptoms as the person who has just died, they are less likely to become obsessed about them and more likely to discount them. If they can be effectively reassured the symptoms can quite quickly disappear. I recently had a woman in my office who was exhibiting every sign of stomach cancer – her husband had just died of it and her pains were the same as his had been. They were very real and very distressing but when I was able to convince her that they were actually imaginary, they disappeared and she began to get better.'

The unexpected and apparently symptomless manner of Adam's death preyed deeply on my mind. It seemed impossible that it could strike with so little warning. There had never been any misgivings about my own heart and I had taken great comfort from a doctor once telling me that I had an 'athlete's heart' with a very slow beat. In the months following Adam's death however I became uneasily aware that all was not well with me for my heart was beating very irregularly. Lying in bed at night I would listen to it drumming in my ears, terrified in case it suddenly stopped like an overwound watch. It had a tendency to race wildly and suddenly lurch to what seemed like an interminable stop – the reaction was an alarming fluttering in my neck and an even faster beating when it decided to restart. Often I was afraid to lie down and go to sleep in case it stopped suddenly and I would never waken again. This heart irregularity was, I am sure, started by the state of stress under which I was then living but by concentrating and brooding on it so much, I effectively managed to damage a healthy heart. It never occurred to me that if I took things calmly and treated my heart flutters as an inevitable reaction to my husband's death from a heart attack, they might have disappeared in time. Instead I denied my natural feelings and threw myself into frenzied activity. I was afraid to stop for a minute in case my caged misery would stalk up on me and hit me in the guts.

Because I felt so tired all the time I developed an addiction to black coffee which seemed to give me the surge of energy that I craved. What I was doing was of course exacerbating my trouble and the heart flutters grew worse from the unnatural rush of adrenalin. The coffee speeded me up like a junkie. Before long a pot full of acrid black coffee had a permanent place on the side of my stove. It could never be sufficiently black, strong or bitter for me and when other people tasted my favourite brew, they screwed up their faces in disgust.

While the coffee was doing its damage, I began to rely more on alcohol than I had ever done before. I needed it to counteract the over-exciting effects of the coffee. It seemed that a couple of gins could drive the heart flutters into abeyance but I did not realize that my respite was only temporary and before very long, the suffering would be worse. Red wine and brandy proved to be very upsetting and I learned to avoid them completely but it still was essential for me to have a few drinks to get through the day. Sometimes in mid morning, I would feel so ill and so desperate that I had to make a trip to the corner cupboard and take a swift sherry out of one of the bottles there. The drink drove my fears and anxieties temporarily into their corner. I had no fear of becoming an alcoholic although I realized that I was depending more and more on drink – 'I can easily do without them,' I told myself, but that argument was self-deception. I was lucky because I have a fairly weak liver and if I take too much alcohol I am violently sick. The dreadful feeling that brings is enough to make me strictly ration my alcohol intake now.

It is however terribly easy for widowed people to take solace in the bottle. A widower told me how he became 'a bottle-of-Bacardi-a-day man' after his wife's death. This headlong descent into alcoholism was only stopped by the realization of what he was doing to his children and by the loss of his licence when the police stopped him for driving under the influence of drink.

A man who works as a lay preacher among the fishing community of north-east Scotland said that he often had to try to help widows with drink problems and the cases he has come across fall into all age groups. One of the saddest was a young woman in her early twenties whose husband was lost at sea leaving her with two small children to bring up.

'She has been drinking steadily for the past few months,' he told me, 'and when I go round to her house to try to speak to her, she won't answer the door because she is so ashamed. All I see are the faces of the small children looking back out at me through the slit of the letter box. They won't let me in and I know their mother is lying drunk inside the house. I've tackled her about it but she always says I don't understand the relief that drink brings because I am a teetotaller myself. It is all because she is so lonely of course. I got her to go to the doctor about her problem but the cure was only temporary and she soon slipped back again. I don't know what is to be done about her.'

The tragic girl, shut up in her home with two little children and a bottle, is not uncommon though the dependence on alcohol is more usual among an older age group than the one to which she belongs. People whose hope for life dies with their partner often opt for a drink-fuddled haze instead of a cold awareness of loneliness. By clever subterfuge they manage to conceal their drinking from friends and family until it has become too deep-rooted a dependence to shake off. They hide the empty bottles and put on a bright face for visitors. One widow in her seventies, who shared a home with her daughter and son-in-law, regularly smuggled half bottles of whisky into the house in her handbag. The half bottle is the giveaway sign of the secret drinker because it can be easily concealed in a pocket or a shopping bag. She began drinking in the morning and by lunchtime she was cheerfully fuddled. In the afternoon it was her habit to go out shopping for the next day's supply and her daughter would watch her skipping about among the cars on the busy road outside their house and say with admiration, 'Just look at her, she is not a bit afraid of all the cars.'

In fact the old lady was too drunk to care. By evening she would be sunk in such a state of maudlin confusion that she retired to bed early and the family had little idea of how she was actually living.

'I have a splendid mother-in-law,' said her daughter's husband. 'She is always cheerful and never in the way.'

When she died of a liver complaint the family were shocked to find her bedroom cupboard and wardrobe full of empty bottles. It was difficult for them to believe that widowhood had turned a previously abstemious and highly respectable woman into a problem drinker. So difficult that when a doctor who was trying to find out the cause of her last illness asked if she ever drank, the family were emphatic that she did not.

'I never remember my mother taking more than a couple of glasses of sherry at Christmas time before my father died,' said her distraught daughter.

As well as ruining their health with coffee and alcohol or with pills and tranquillizers, widowed people sometimes find that their physical appearance deteriorates dramatically during grieving. The old story about hair going grey overnight may be exaggerated but other ageing signs can certainly be accelerated for the face is a good indicator of the state of mind. A few weeks after Adam's death I suddenly noticed that a series of fine lines had appeared round my mouth. They had not been there as far as I knew when he was alive but now they were so deeply engraved that they looked as if I had had them forever. Twisting and grimacing my face I discovered which expression brought them on – it was when I tried to bite my lips to prevent them trembling. They were the lines of bitten-back tears. As the years have progressed and the need for weeping has become less pressing, the mouth lines have softened and become less obvious. They are still there, but like my sorrow which is still with me too, they have ceased to make such an obvious impression on me.

An artist friend who met me recently said, 'I can see that you are happier now.'

When asked how he knew, the answer was, 'It's in your face, the lines all turn up but they used to turn down.'

And it is true, watching the people around me when they are unaware of the scrutiny, it is possible to tell those who are really happy and those who are only putting on a brave front. At moments of unawareness their state of mind shows in their faces.

Stress can manifest itself in other ways than bringing wrinkles to the face. In the morning when I woke up just after Adam died, I used to find my hands knuckled tightly into fists and sometimes the marks of my fingernails would be in the palms for a long time afterwards. Unknown to me I was also holding my jaw clenched like a boxer about to take a punch, the back teeth bit down on each other and the muscle along the cheekbone was always tense. I did not realize this continual strain until I read a book about relaxation techniques and learned how to unloosen the tension in the face and jaw. Think about it yourself, close your eyes and concentrate on your face. Is your jaw tense, is your forehead tight? Think your forehead wide and wider, feel it relax and allow that unloosening of tension to extend to the rest of your facial muscles. The feeling of peace it brings is remarkable.

The next physical manifestation I had of post-bereavement stress was an ugly rash that appeared on my face and neck. It was quickly followed by an outbreak on my hands and wrists which I thought was an infection brought about by touching the face rash. I was acutely conscious of those unsightly blotches and tried to cover them up with long sleeves, high necks and make-up but any upset or agitation made them flare redder than ever. A prescribed ointment had little effect and quite quickly my hands became so infected that it was painful to wear any rings. I have always been vain about my hands and love large rings but the rash was so persistent I had to give them up altogether. It was difficult for me to take off my wedding ring however because it represented my link with Adam. I clung to it for months and was forever scratching away at the ugly rash that surrounded it. One day I could bear the pain no longer and took it off. Miraculously from that time my rashes cleared up. Today I can wear rings again – but not my wedding ring. If I put it on the rash comes back. In its place I wear an eternity ring that Adam gave me when our son was born. In a way it represents something different than the wedding ring – something more permanent and less illusory.

Some years after the rashes disappeared I read a newspaper article about 'wedding ring eczema' – an irritating itch that appeared on the wedding ring finger of a sufferer. It was discovered that invariably they were people who were going through a troubled phase in their marriage – and the rash appeared even if they were not consciously aware of their marital troubles at the time. I think that my rash was wedding ring eczema and it was an unconscious cry to be rid of the links with the past and all the pain they brought me. Inside I longed to be happy again but I was also guilty at my need to forget what had happened. To find a cure all I had to do was to summon up enough bravery to take my wedding ring off and that was a huge step, a huge disloyalty at the time. Rationalizing all this of course is a later development for it is much easier to see one's problems in retrospect.

As the months went on my heart flutters grew worse and I became convinced that they were symptoms of a serious disease.

I was however unable to consult a doctor about them because I was afraid of being told that I too was soon to die and leave my children alone and unprotected. My reactions to this were illogical but I could not bring myself to have the tremors properly diagnosed. A strange coincidence however forced me into direct action.

That winter I started doing research in the India Office Library because I conceived the idea of writing an article about some of the remarkable women who lived in India in the eighteenth and nineteenth centuries. One afternoon a library assistant brought me a cardboard box of old letters.

'These might interest you,' she said. 'No one has ever done any work on them but I had a glance at them recently and they look very interesting.'

The letters dated from the mid 1790s to the first decade of the nineteenth century and they had been written from Madras by two sisters to another sister and their mother in London. The Madras based sisters had gone to the East with the husband of one of them. He was a judge in the employ of the East India Company and his wife had taken her younger sister along with her as a companion and in the hope of finding her a suitable husband.

The sisters were very different: the younger one, Poppy, was flirtatious and frivolous, interested in little more than re-laying the more scandalous items of gossip back to her family in London and sending long shopping lists of food and finery to be forwarded on to Madras; the married sister, Elizabeth, won my complete regard for she knew and loved the country in which she found herself. The descriptions she gave of Madras life in the eighteenth century enthralled me because it had differed so little in essentials from the life I knew myself in up-country India. I was amazed to learn how little it had changed over nearly two centuries. Elizabeth was a bluestocking who learned to read and write several Indian languages and who also pursued a serious study of botany and zoology. There was no trace of the overbearing 'mem sahib' about her and she described the native life and customs without racial prejudice or blinkered conviction that the ways of the West are always best. She spent her afternoons dissecting birds on the veranda of her bungalow – much to the surprise of her servants – and she struck up a friendship with a German botanist who was more to her taste as a companion than the frivolous gamblers that hung around the house of Lord Clive, the governor of Madras. The German botanist named a flower after her and it is still listed in botanical books with her surname. The description given to it is 'tender and reclusive' and I feel that is a compliment paid to her by her courtly German admirer.

She had need of kindness because her marriage was not happy. She longed for a child but was unable to conceive and her longings were made worse by frequent news of another pregnancy for Mary, her sister. Unfortunately each pregnancy except the last ended in miscarriage and Elizabeth in Madras grieved for each one as if it had been her own. Her husband, Henry, was an overbearing boor unable to appreciate her sensitivity and shyness which he could only see as a drawback to his own career. As the years passed he left her more and more to her own devices, living in a bungalow several miles outside the city of Madras and only coming to visit her at weekends. She sank into hypochondria and illness. One of her letters home described physical symptoms she was suffering, symptoms that mirrored my own, a sudden stopping of the heart and a 'fluttering' in the neck. She called them her 'spasms'. She had asked her sister for advice about them but of course no replies were included in the box of letters. On the afternoon that I reached the last letter in the box, I did not at first realize it was written in a different hand.

I saw it was posted from Cape Town and thought, 'Oh, thank goodness, she is on her way home. She will see her family again.' Then the querulous tone of the letter struck me, complaining about everything and especially about expense – 'everything here is so dear,' and finally adding, 'troubles have piled on me of late.' The signature was that of Elizabeth's husband. What had happened to her? Surely fate had not been so cruel as to allow her to die in India? I searched in dread for her obituary in the columns of the Madras newspapers and sure enough, there it was, a tiny mention at the foot of a column with none of the fulsome descriptions that were awarded to other people of her status in the tiny European community of that time. She had been buried, I read, in a church which I have once visited. I realized how stupid it was to grieve for a woman dead so long ago but coming on her death that way intensified the shock and grief that I was already suffering. I left the library in tears and never went back. My heart flutters from that time grew worse and not a day went by without me being startled and frightened by them. Had they killed my friend of so long ago, I wondered?

I have always dreaded illness because at five years old I was confined to bed for almost a year with bronchitis and pneumonia. The memory of that long invalidism gave me a great fear of doctors and of ever being ill again, so much so that I would go to great lengths to conceal symptoms from any doctor I had to consult, even as an adult. To this day I am not sure if I am free of that irrational fear. The worry about the heart flutters and my fear that the children would be orphaned, however, eventually forced me to seek medical help but even then I could not be frank and was fobbed off with more tranquillizers. During my visit to the doctor however I had asked his advice about what could have been wrong with the subject of my researches. He listened to the symptoms and said, 'It could have been the menopause. It could have been a bad heart or she could have been showing the first symptoms of a brain tumour.'

As can be expected that diagnosis only made my own heart flutters worse and they grew so bad that I was having them almost continually.

My eventual crack-up was sudden and dramatic. One morning while I was attempting to hoover the carpets, I simply collapsed on the floor and lay there watching rivulets of sweat course down my arms and off the ends of my fingers. My face too was so wet with sweat that I could hardly see. Outside the rain poured down the window panes in sympathy because it was my wicked month, November. A friend called as I lay there in a heap and taking one look went straight to the phone and called a doctor. From there, by a progression of events, I was given an appointment to attend the cardiac clinic at the local general hospital and even before I went for the tests I had an overwhelming sense of relief because my fears had been revealed and something was going to be done about them. A weight had been lifted from me already. My mood between having the test and receiving the results can only be described as stoic. Eventually the cardiac specialist told me that I was suffering from an abnormally fast heart beat and pills were to be prescribed for me. That was all the explanation he was prepared to give for he obviously belonged to the school of medical opinion that thinks the less a patient knows the better, especially if she is an obviously hysterical woman. At no time did he make any investigation into why I was hysterical or what were the circumstances behind my illness and I am sure that they were a very important contributing factor.

As I was gathering up my handbag to leave his office, I summoned up enough courage to ask, 'How long do I have to take the pills?'

'Providing there are no side effects forever.'

'What sort of side effects?'

'You will know if you have them,' was my dismissal, but as I went through the door he vouchsafed something else: 'My advice to you, however, is change your way of life.'

His parting shot rang in my ears. Change your way of life. How could I stop worrying and grieving and racing around like a rat in a trap? It seemed impossible. How easy it was for that dry and dusty-looking man in the white coat to hand out advice without giving any guidelines about how it could be followed when your whole life was literally in chaos. While I was fumbling in my pocket for the car keys, I put my newly prescribed bottle of pink pills on the roof and suddenly the thought struck me that he had in fact found something terribly wrong with my heart and because he was too kind to tell me, had just sent me out with a bottle of placebos to deceive me. But he had not looked kind and he had not acted kind, Aloud to the empty air I asked, 'But it will soon be Christmas. Surely he wouldn't let me die for Christmas?'

The absurdity of the thought made me laugh out loud at my own foolishness and then I realized that I was at some sort of crossroads. Standing in that dingy car park I knew that if I was going to survive, I would have to reappraise my situation. It was no longer possible to go on living in the past with its agonizing memories. Perhaps that was the moment when my recovery began.

# 5

# The Siamese Twin Syndrome

IT is only when the widowed reach the stage of realizing that they must make a new life for themselves that they are fully conscious of what can only be described as the Siamese Twin Syndrome.

This was most succinctly described for me by a woman talking about how she felt when her husband died: 'I felt as if I was a Siamese twin that had lost its brother.'

Some of the most evocative descriptions of widowing come from people who talk about the sensation of actual physical separation that bereavement brings: 'It was like losing half of myself,' and 'It was as if I had been chopped in two.'

This feeling of surgical cutting off is at times almost overwhelming and it affects the mind as well as the body. For my own part I really felt as if I had been split down the middle like a bit of wood. Through the years of marriage, almost without realizing it, Adam and I had grown together like a knotted vine and the cutting away of one part almost killed the other. I was left with all my broken parts exposed, told to go on functioning with what was left.

A widow told me how she felt: 'I thought I was about to die myself. For the first year, I had the most terrible bone aching tiredness as if I was functioning on only half of the resources that were necessary. I carried the tiredness around like a knapsack on my back and I thought that if I managed to get to bed early and have a lot of sleep, things would get better but they never did.

'All the time my legs hurt and the calves ached and quivered continually. For a little while in the morning I had enough energy but as the day wore on I grew more and more exhausted until by teatime I was in a state of physical collapse. A short walk to the shops or to collect my daughter from school was like a marathon run for me. I was terrified in case I collapsed on the pavement and I could imagine myself lying there, an untidy and undignified heap with a lot of strangers staring at me.

'When I did get up enough courage to go shopping, I would be overcome with a terrible, sweating panic half-way there so I'd have to turn round and go home again. I'd make up all sorts of excuses, even to myself, saying I'd forgotten my purse or thought I'd left the gas on. It was terrible.

'Eventually I did all my shopping with the car because I felt safe inside it. I'd double park or stop on yellow lines and dash into the shops to buy the food we needed. Once back in the car it was like being safe in my private cave and the shaking and trembling would stop.

'What was really terrible was having to stand in a supermarket checkout queue – if it was too long I'd begin to feel faint and my eyes would go out of focus. One day the panic was so overpowering that I just walked away and left my loaded trolley standing there in the queue. I was so ashamed that I was never able to go back to that particular shop again. We used to do the family shopping on late night Fridays so that the children could go with me. I always insisted on pushing the trolley because it made me feel better having something to hold on to.'

In time by fighting her terrors and being aware of what was causing them – her feelings of loss and bereavement – she managed to lead a normal life again.

'A terror recognized is a terror half conquered,' she said.

A widower who had lost his right arm in the war gave the most graphic description of the feeling of being left maimed by bereavement. He gestured to his empty sleeve and said simply, 'Losing my wife was like losing this. Part of you disappears and you know you will never be able to get it back. For the rest of your life you will be functioning on what is left.'

Significantly he had not had an artificial arm fitted nor had he remarried.

'If I can describe what I mean,' he went on, 'it would be to compare the loss of my wife with the shock I felt when my arm was amputated. I still felt as if it was there for a long time after it had been taken away.

'I remember that when I came out of hospital a friend offered to teach me to play tennis again because I had been a pretty good player before the war. The problem was that for a long time – for years in fact – I kept on trying to hit the ball with the hand that was no longer there. That is the best illustration of what life as a widower has been like. I'm hitting the ball with a non-existent arm. I have to keep on reminding myself that she is dead even though it happened twelve years ago. In the beginning I used to think almost every day, "Just wait till I get home and tell that to Alice," and with a shock I'd have to remember that she was no longer there. If there's a good joke or something interesting happens, I still occasionally find myself thinking I'd like to share it with her. It's particularly bad if there is a big success or a good business deal – there's no one to share it with any more and often I have to pull myself up and remember that.'

But everyone has the chance of rebuilding a life and that rebuilding means that they have to create a new part of themselves to replace what has been lost. What they replace it with depends very much on the adjustment they make to their bereavement and to the conscious effort they put into the process of recreation. The sign that this is going on comes when people who have been widowed for a while will suddenly realize – 'I don't think I would like to be married again.'

A young widow explained how she felt. 'I wouldn't want to be a wife again because I have grown used to doing so many things on my own and taking my own decisions. I suppose it makes you very selfish really. I don't want to lose this independence that I have gained.'

She had grown another half to replace what had been lost and she was one of the fortunate people who were happy with what she had become. The process of regrowth is very gradual and while it is going on you are not aware of it, but my own realization came one day when I suddenly wondered, 'If Adam was to come back would he like me as I am now?'

Because of course I am a very different person from the woman who received the news of his death.

The anti-Royalist MP Willie Hamilton, who remarried when he was in his early sixties after nearly fourteen years of widowhood, reflected on the changes in personality that widowing brings.

'For a long time, after I had got used to the idea of being on my own, I actually quite enjoyed being a widower. There was no one to whom I had to answer; no one that I was afraid of having let down by anything I did. My first wife and family had to put up with a lot because of the things I said in Parliament and sometimes when I was going home I'd think, "Oh dear, how will I explain *that*?" When I was a widower there was no one to bother about except myself and I must admit I liked that.

'But as I grew older I began to realize how very much on my own I was. I live in a nice block of flats with pleasant neighbours but there is not anyone around who I could have called on for help if anything happened or if I got ill. I thought to myself, "You'd better do something about this." So I got married again.'

His story is a succinct summing up of many people's experiences. Widowhood when you are living a full and active life is actually a kind of liberation but few people look forward to a life of loneliness as they grow older. If remarriage is not likely – and it is less possible for women than for men – then steps have to be taken while life is still good to lay down the basis for a fulfilling and interesting old age – friendships have to be made, interests pursued, lifestyles organized with care and attention. It is always a danger to let things drift hoping that 'something will turn up'. Remember even Mr Micawber's luck ran out eventually.

One of my grandmothers was ninety-three when she died and until the last year of her life she had been extremely fit and active. What caused her to collapse was the sudden realization of her age because for years she had been telling us she was eighty-three – when she reached that age she simply stopped counting. Then one day a man wanting to check on her pension book told her the real age and the shock was so terrible that she took to her bed that afternoon and never got up, dying a year later. I was furious with her for this abdication and used to exhort her to get up because time was a purely artificial concept – her day was the same as mine. But she did not listen of course.

When the widowed start rebuilding their lives it is important first of all to keep healthy. Many widowed people stop cooking proper food for themselves, gradually slipping into a diet of tins and frozen food eaten off a tray in front of the television set. It no longer seems worthwhile to cut down their smoking or to keep up hobbies. Anyone whose tennis partner has been their dead wife or husband finds it only too easy never to go near a tennis court again. People who used to go walking together with their partner often find it easy to sit at home with their feet on the fireplace, brooding over the past. If sports or pastimes are too painful because of the memories they bring, something new should be found to take their place.

It takes determination but everyone would find it beneficial to do a few simple exercises every day if they do not have a particular sport. Five or ten minutes spent touching the toes or rotating from the waist can keep you in trim; even people in their eighties can benefit from a simple regimen of exercise. It is easy to do your exercises in the shower when the warm water pouring over you takes away the strain on the muscles. In time exercises become as essential a part of the daily routine as cleaning the teeth and if they are forgotten, the omission is very obvious quite quickly. It is important, however, to do the exercises every day because slipping becomes easier than practice and giving up is a general temptation. By nature I am a slipper and when I forget to do my exercises I always find the strain and pain when I once again return to them not worth the luxury of lying in bed for ten minutes longer and forgetting about them.

There are literally dozens of books about simple exercises, and women's magazines always run regular features about how to keep yourself in trim. It is important, however, not to be too ambitious at first – just take it very easy. Exercises like the US Marine regime which was popular a few years ago, although they were publicized as being possible for both men and women, actually raised the blood pressure and could for certain people be dangerous.

Another useful way of keeping yourself in trim is to do yoga. It is a common misconception that yoga involves convoluted exercises that involve standing on the head and winding the legs round the neck. Older people very rightly imagine that they would never be able to do anything like that. In fact yoga can be as taxing and muscle stretching as you care to make it and a good teacher will always make sure that everyone proceeds at their own pace. There have been numerous instances of people well into pensionable age taking up yoga for the first time with great benefit to their health. One of the big advantages about yoga is the tranquillity of mind it can bring, especially when you learn the breathing exercises. I learned it in India from an Indian teacher called Professor Bhatt who for years had taught stiff European ladies the principles of yoga. He was a great psychologist and gave each pupil an individual list of exercises which he knew they could accomplish without too much trouble. I never learned to stand on my head for example. But I did learn how to control my breathing and how to go into a state of relaxation so profound that I almost felt as if I was floating outside my body. Yoga classes are readily available and well worth trying especially if you feel nervous and tense. The breathing exercises alone will help to calm you down.

It is always best to do yoga under the eye of a teacher and in a class because it is not a discipline that people find easy to continue on their own. I regret I let my yoga slip several years before I was widowed because I know that if I had been doing it during my bad years, my reactions to the various problems that I encountered would have been different.

Recently, I have become interested in relaxation and meditation. People often think that relaxation is simply lying down and closing the eyes but in fact you have to make a conscious effort to relax every part of your body and to slow down the racing around of your mind. Anyone who has a busy life and a demanding schedule would very quickly find that the time they spend meditating is amply repaid by the increased acuteness of their mind and work output when they finish their session. Meditation is known to lower the blood pressure and soothe away mental turmoil. It is now being recommended for people suffering from hypertension and heart trouble. There are some very good books on meditating and relaxation techniques and I have found a cassette in which a teacher talks you through a relaxation session extremely useful.

In widowhood appearance should not be neglected – in fact this is a time when you need the solace of looking good because your ego takes a terrible blow when someone who has been your lifelong protector and admirer is suddenly removed. It is so easy for someone in grief to stop worrying about their weight and to seek solace in fattening food – a box of chocolates consumed in one sitting is a way of satisfying internal longing. And with sugar addiction the more you eat of it, the more you want.

It is also easy to put off having your hair done in case you panic about having to sit for a long time in the hairdresser's. A woman who found it impossible to stay calm in a hairdressing salon after her husband died did not have her hair cut for two years until her farouche appearance forced her to snap out of her fears and inertia. Buying new clothes can sometimes be difficult from a financial point of view but making new social contacts is important, and people who do not know your sad story will not be likely to think well of you if you straggle around fat and unlovely in unkempt clothes. But how easy it is to slip into an uncaring way of life when it seems that taking yourself in hand is a waste of time for no one cares about you any more.

It is much easier to rebuild your life if there is someone apart from yourself to worry about. The widow and widower with children are held to their responsibilities by the demands of their families – children have to be taken out, they have to be cared for and parents have to be presentable on special occasions for the child's sake.

Even when children are grown up and away from home, widowed people often find a focus for their love and attention in grandchildren who can be taken out to parks or museums and who can be talked to. Grandchildren are a wonderful focus for passing on one's thoughts and theories and this relationship can be a very close one.

I am not however advocating that widowed people should sink their lives in children or grandchildren. That is a terrible mistake and can often result in even greater misery because children need their own lives and they must eventually cast off their links and leave. They can also inhibit their parents' lives unnecessarily. Widows in particular feel tied by their children who can even impose celibacy on their mother – 'The children would not like it if I took a man home,' said more than one woman.

It is best for children – at least when they are older – to realize that their mother or father is a flesh and blood person with natural desires and drives. The acknowledgement of this often puts family relationships on a better, more honest footing.

As far as the enhancement of life in widowhood is concerned, I am a great advocate of keeping pets. Psychologists have found that people with pets are less likely to become disturbed or isolated. One of the prescriptions often given to people recovering from heart attacks is to get a cat or a dog. The presence of the animal in a household not only has a soothing effect but stroking their fur can actually induce a feeling of peace and contentment and lower blood pressure.

The keeping of a pet in widowhood means that demands are made on the owner – cats, dogs and cage birds all have to be fed, kept clean and taken to the vet when they are ill. They can be spoken to and confided in – problems articulated are never so bad as those that roll continually around in your head. Dogs are my preferred domestic pets because they make greater demands on their owner than cats or birds. Several widowed women have said, 'I couldn't keep a dog because I could never get away if I had one.' That excuse does not hold water in many cases because often the people who plead it hardly go anywhere anyway and if they did have a dog it is always possible either to board it out during an absence or find a friend who will look after it. Striking up acquaintances is always easier if you own a dog for people will stop and admire a puppy. A spinster who had lived a petless existence for many years and suddenly bought herself a puppy said, 'I am simply astonished at how many people in this road who never spoke to me before have stopped and talked about my dog. I have made a lot of new friends because of it.'

A young mother with a baby and a dog remarked that when she took the baby out in its pram without the dog, hardly anyone talked to her. If she took the dog along as well, she had several friendly conversations on the way.

'I think a lot of people in this country are more into animals than they are into children,' she said. But there is perhaps another explanation. People who would like to talk to others are often tongue-tied. The chance to stop and pat a dog and to pass a few words about it is a good way of breaking the social ice.

Dogs also need exercising – another way of keeping fit. For as long as I can remember there have never been less than two dogs in my family. When I was born I was given as a present a mongrel puppy called Toby who had the same birthday as I did and I grew up with him as a loved friend. I was sure that he was all-wise and all-seeing and when he died, aged over fourteen years, I was sick with weeping.

Every dog I have owned I can remember vividly and not always with unmitigated pleasure – manic bull terriers head my list of dogs I would not like to meet again. But others are remembered with greater affection.

They are the recipients of my most private thoughts and I will often walk about talking to them while they sit, heads cocked, drinking it all in. Dogs are a great wall against which to bounce your ideas.

An old widow told me very sadly, 'The thing I miss most about being alone is never going dancing. It is twenty-five years since I danced and I used to love it.'

I love dancing too and since Adam died there have been few opportunities for social dancing but some time ago a woman artist who is a friend told me about how she relaxes during concentrated painting sessions. She puts on a record and dances away on her own round the floor of her studio.

'I dance and dance and it makes me feel marvellous. When it is over I can go back to working with new ideas,' she said.

I copied her tip and found it works for me too. When work hits a block, I often get up and dance round the kitchen like a lumpen Pavlova and my dogs love this – they prance round me with their tongues lolling out and their paws raised like a couple of acolytes, and I can tell by their faces that they are laughing fit to burst. We must make a strange sight – a miniature dachshund, a fat white mongrel and me attempting our own version of *Swan Lake*. Dogs have a great talent for allowing you to make a fool of yourself in front of them.

On a more mundane level, it is also valuable for people on their own to keep a dog as protection, especially in the city. My mongrel Patch is convinced that her function in life is to guard the house and I don't need a doorbell because she hears every footfall on the path. She would certainly attack anyone unwise enough to enter the house in my absence and at night with Patch asleep on the foot of my bed, I feel as safe as someone with a personal bodyguard. The row of houses in which we lived in London was a notorious attraction for burglars – every one of them except us was burgled and one of the neighbours was broken into three times in five years. A policeman told me that our amazing exemption from the attention of thieves was probably due to our dogs, Ham and Phoebe, who set up a terrible baying behind the front door when anyone came near the house. What the burglars did not know was that Ham had no teeth and Phoebe was so eager to be loved that she would have led them all over the house. They made a lot of noise however and that was all that was necessary to deter the thieves from making their acquaintance.

In fact our immunity from burglaries might also have been due to the fact that I made friends with a burglar. He was a young man who came to adult education classes in creative writing which I taught in the first couple of years of my widowhood. He was a poet, and it turned out, better at versifying than at burgling because half-way through the class he disappeared for a stretch inside one of Her Majesty's prisons. However, he adopted me and my family and told me that he had put the word round his friends 'Lay off number 15'. It is doubtful if his criminal connections could have extended to every burglar in south-east London but along with my dogs he must share the kudos for surrounding our house with a cordon sanitaire. I still remember my burglar poet with affection and hanging on the wall of my office is a yellowing poem he wrote to me from one of his prison cells entitled 'To Elizabeth'.

Researches among widows of my own generation however proved to me how many of them are thrown into a vortex of ignorance and inadequacy when their men die. They have no idea how to organize their own lives because they have always relied on someone else to do it for them – many of them have never paid the bills, argued with tradesmen or even driven a car.

They have been feather-bedded all their lives and can hardly moan about their lot when they arrive at widowhood without any skills. The number of women who said almost with pride that they were unable to drive particularly appalled me – all their travelling was done as passengers. Driving is as essential a skill in the modern world as knowing how to use the telephone and it should be taught at school or by parents to their children as a matter of course.

For women who have always relied on men, the state of widowhood is acutely frightening and they are the people who can most benefit from a new training in assertiveness. Classes in this are taught at some evening institutes or in university extra-mural classes around the country and there is an excellent handbook, *Self Assertion for Women* by Pamela E. Butler published by Harper and Row.

The training teaches women how to accept compliments with grace; how to fend for themselves in situations of sexual harassment; how to cope with unscrupulous tradesmen or people who are prepared to put them down because 'she's only a woman'. Few women are born assertive – they have to learn it. Many women who think of themselves as assertive are actually just bulldozing bullies, for assertiveness of the best kind is not aggression but a system of 'give and take' – the business of finding an acceptable medium in every fraught situation.

The classes in Edinburgh are held by a girl called Laila Kjellstrom, who takes a group of eight women once a week for ten weeks, either in local institutes or in the University's Extramural Department. She teaches them how to build up their own self-esteem, how to argue without growing angry, how to stand up for themselves without being 'aggressive' in the worst sense of the word. They learn that if someone criticizes you, the right thing to do is to think about whether they have any basis for what they are saying and why they say it. The classes are given 'homework' to do . . . exercises like saying 'no' to an awkward request, or not making a sacrifice of themselves for their husbands and families. She reported to me that the women who attended her classes were very enthusiastic about the results of the exercises and they felt, for the first time in their lives in many cases, that it was not a crime to put their own interests first.

She said, 'There are still situations in which I know that I am not assertive myself but at least I can recognize them.'

One of my own golden rules for difficult situations I remembered from Adam when he was talking about business deals with difficult clients – 'I always remember that I have to leave the other chap an acceptable way out.' This has proved useful in taking me through some very rough water.

The teachers of assertiveness training all said that widows made up a large proportion of their pupils and one of these told me how much she had benefited from taking the course: 'I was totally at sea. I didn't know how to live on my own,' she said, 'but going to the classes has made me think that life alone is possible after all.'

However, going to classes and practising assertiveness for homework is not really necessary if a woman is determined to prove that she can stand on her own feet and is also able to ask friends for support when she needs it. It is not necessary to throw yourself on other people or to be feather-bedded in their concern – no one need lose their self-determination or become a burden just because they are widowed. The giving and receiving of sympathy is not inhibiting to recovery for its healing and reassuring powers are very necessary in the beginning. The bereaved should remember, however, that once having proved they can stand alone, they must learn to walk unaided.

# 6

# *The Problems*

THERE are three main areas where problems arise in widowhood – money, the children and sex.

### *Money*

Because I am a Scot I have never thought it indelicate to bring up the subject of money but this attitude is not always shared by the English who would far rather tell you about their sex life than their bank balance. In fact I have found that the only English people who regularly plead poverty and talk fearfully of their financial situation are those who have more than enough money for their needs. However, it is necessary to introduce a mercenary note here because money is of paramount importance to the widowed, especially to widowed women.

It has been reliably estimated that in more than 90 per cent of widowings, a woman's financial circumstances change for the worse and sometimes dramatically so. The rich widow is generally a character of fiction, although in America it has become almost part of the marriage contract for a man to provide himself with generous insurance policies so that his wife can collect when he dies. In Britain, however, it is generally expected and regarded as fitting for a widow's rightful expectation to be a degree of financial as well as physical and emotional deprivation. The 'rich widow' is almost a term of denigration. A married woman said complacently on the subject of widows:

'They are always pleading poverty but you only have to go to a seaside resort and you see busloads full of them.'

What she overlooked was that the busloads of widows were probably old age pensioners on an Evergreen Outing. Not for the British widow the luxury tour of the capitals of Europe but an afternoon in rainy Clacton.

The day I received my husband's last pay cheque I abruptly realized that I was probably going to spend the rest of my life permanently hard up. The only sure bastion against starvation was my pension book for widowed mothers and because Adam had worked a large part of his career in India and had therefore not stamped an insurance card in Britain we were allotted only a 74 per cent pension. For six months widows were given a double pension every week to tide them over the first part of widowing but on the day I was suddenly on the basic level of pension, I was forced to realize that your basic income is well below the national average – I had joined the ranks of the paupers.

Of course everyone's problems are comparative and there were very many people much worse off than I was. The trouble with always having lived well, however, is that you get used to a way of life that costs quite a lot of money – you have your own car, you buy the odd bottle of wine if someone is coming to supper, you take the children to the cinema or for a special outing, you buy them new shoes, not shoes from a jumble sale that some other child has worn before.

Because of the intervention of my husband's previous employer and the immense help of our newly acquired lawyer, Adam's employers were prevailed upon to settle a sum of money on me and the children because Adam had died in their service and they had him insured against such an eventuality. This they would only do however if it was tied up in such a way that I was not empowered to touch the capital. The Taylor Trust Fund was to be established. It sounds very imposing but the title was a great deal more important than the actuality because as I was told by one of the financial advisers, 'Of course it's far from large as trust funds go. You're not at all rich in the true meaning of the word.' He meant our trust fund was peanuts.

The company were however treating me with the suspicion that is awarded to the widow, especially if she is still fairly young. If I were to get my hands on the money, what was to prevent me blowing the lot on fast cars and gigolos? What if I rushed off to the Riviera and left all my children to starve? They reckoned, 'This woman has never done anything in her life to warrant our confidence. Her husband died without making a will. Was there perhaps some reason why he did not do so? Is she perhaps unstable, flighty, unreliable? We had better not take a chance with *our* money.' The lump sum they informed me was to be invested in 'safe' stocks and shares and the income paid out to me at so much a month. Any capital expenditure would have to be approved of by a committee of bankers, a lawyer, a stockbroker and two trustees – of which I was one. I had the privilege awarded to me of being able to pick my co-trustee. I chose my friend Lorna.

For one thing, I reckoned, I needed another woman to be on my side against the faceless men of the City. She would be more likely to appreciate any problems I encountered. Secondly, she was herself a successful business-woman who could not fail to impress my new financial keepers and this turned out to be the case.

We were summoned to a meeting in the head office of a bank in the City to have all arrangements explained to us and to meet the bankers who were to administer the money. Lorna and I sat at one end of a long, highly polished table while the men clustered at the other, nodding wisely over company portfolios. They asked me my age and when I told them – forty – they put their heads together and one said, 'Well, gentlemen, here we are dealing with a twenty-five-year trust.'

They were putting a date on my possible death! The money would have to be tied up until then. If my children were to look forward to riches it would only come with my funeral. And what riches. The investments that are made on behalf of trusts have to be rock sure and these are the ones that yield small returns. When all the arrangements were made I ended up with a total yearly payment of less than one quarter of the money that Adam had earned. As the years have passed the trust income has shrunk considerably because of inflation, and today the income from the investments is not sufficient to run my car.

But of course the fact that we even had a quarter of the money that came into the house before our wage earner died put us into a privileged category. The efforts of our kindly lawyer also meant that money was released from the trust fund capital to pay the death duties on the house and we were able to stay in our home. As far as widowed families went we were very lucky. Today we look back with horror on the tales of Dickensian misery in Victorian times but we forget that there are still people living in equal – if less dramatic and colourful – poverty today.

Over 336,000 single parent families in Britain today exist on supplementary benefit and they are well and truly caught in the poverty trap because any effort to improve their position means that the benefit is cut. The description 'single parent' is in itself depressing because it has connotations of trouble and deprivation – single parent families seem to have the heavy end of the stick in every respect and much has been written about their disadvantages, so much so that even when they have no problems, they begin to think that they should. We are told that children from single parent families are more likely to become ill, do badly at school, need treatment for psychological upsets than those from a two parent family. We are told that statistics prove that children with only one parent are more likely to end up in court or be placed under probation orders. A sole parent trying to bring up a family is haunted by the problems that wait round every corner because of the awful 'single parent' label.

Much of the trouble of course arises from lack of money. The average single parent with one child living on Income Support receives a total payment of just under £85.50 a week from the state. This has to cover rent, rates, transport, clothes, food and electricity so it is not difficult to work out how little is left for frivolities or luxuries.

'So why don't they get a job?' is the inevitable question. But several things militate against this solution. Jobs are not easy to find, especially for women with few skills beyond looking after a house and bringing up their children. They are competing in a cut-throat market against people with better, more recently earned qualifications.

Secondly, when a woman with children goes for a job interview she has only to mention her family to be automatically struck off the list of possibles – employers fear that if the children are sick, the mother will become an absentee, that their needs will be put before the needs of her job. 'I always know that when they ask the question, "And what arrangements will you make for your children?" that I have lost my chance of the job,' said one young widow. 'You see, you can't win. If I tell them that I'll make sure that the children will not stop me giving full attention to my work, they think I'm an unnatural and uncaring woman. If I hesitate and make it sound that I'm only going to trust to luck that the kids will be all right, they immediately think I'll be an absentee in a crisis.'

I know from personal experience the problems of trying to work and look after a family, for even when a child is attending school full time, there are anxious weeks in the holidays and the ever present worry that the child is going to fall sick. Every sniffle, every sneeze makes the working mother anxious. In fact children whose mother has to go out to work often have a better attendance record at school than other families because the luxury of a day in bed with a slight cold is never theirs.

Even such a simple job as escorting children to and from school is an ever present problem for the working mother. Employers do not look kindly on late arrivers or on someone who has to dash out at school closing time to make sure the children cross the road safely. If you live in the city, you can be nearly distracted with worry every day about the dangers to which an unescorted child is exposed. Neighbours who are prepared to help out occasionally feel put upon if asked to do it every day. It is difficult to find someone reliable to take care of your children and, though child minders are available, they are expensive. A widower said that it cost him in excess of £3000 a year for a full-time housekeeper and though a tax allowance for a housekeeper was then allowed for widowers – but not for widows – he was still very much out of pocket.

It is a temptation for the working parent to put the younger children in the care of the oldest in the family but in doing this they often put themselves in danger of breaking the law because no child under the age of sixteen should be left looking after other children. Parents who do it however warn the child in charge not to answer the door and the family grows up in an atmosphere of fear and tension. Some single parents are hag-ridden by the fear that 'they' – nebulous authority – will take their children away. Once the children are put in care of a local authority there can be all sorts of difficulties put in the way of getting them back again.

Most people are very vague in their minds about the exact powers of authority and tend to look on all the social services as well-meaning ogres who are best avoided. Recently the mother of a two-year-old child said that if her daughter fell over and hurt herself, she would keep the child indoors until the bruise cleared up: 'I'm a single parent and they might think I've been hitting her. I don't want my baby taken away from me.' But babies in two parent families fall over and are bruised without anyone thinking a thing about it.

Another widow told of how when her children were small she worked as a cleaner in a block of offices, going out to work at 5 a.m. and getting back at half past seven to get them up for school.

'I used to go out in the morning leaving them asleep in bed and I knew that I was breaking the law but we needed the money so badly. All the time I was at work I used to worry in case one of the children got up and hurt itself or was sick and the others wouldn't know what to do. Every time there was a story in the newspaper or an item on the telly about children being burned to death in a fire I used to burst into tears. I was in a perpetual state of nerves and the children were as bad as me because I infected them with my worries.'

In a book called *Casualties of the Sea* William McFie wrote, 'It is extraordinary how many emotional storms one may weather if one is ballasted by ever so little gold.' The casualties of widowing would certainly find their paths smoother and many of their miseries would disappear if they were more financially secure.

As well as finding themselves without money, many families find that widowing means they no longer have a home. There are many jobs with 'tied houses' – the armed forces, the ministry, some medical practitioners, farm workers and prison officers among them. Though many of those jobs are reasonably well paid and it is the intention of the wage earner to buy a house before retirement, death is not always a respecter of plans and when a man dies young, his widow and children often find themselves having to move with nowhere to go. Around three months is allowed before the family must move out of a tied house but even when there is somewhere ready for them, often they are sad at having to leave the house they have known.

When I was widowed one of the earliest pieces of advice given to me was: 'Don't make any radical plans for at least two years. Just stay put and wait till you are really determined in your mind about what you want to do.'

It was good advice because for the first few years of widowhood, judgement does seem to be erratic and ideas which appear most appealing for a while end up as quite impractical. There is a fairly common widowed syndrome – the wandering widow, who moves around from house to house and place to place in an erratic search for peace of mind. If you are unhappy where you are, you think things will change for the better somewhere else. The wandering widow is happy for about six months after every move until she settles down and the novelty wears off and then she is away on her travels again.

But families who *have* to move house every so often do so reluctantly. A vicar's widow talked of how she had to leave her husband's rectory a couple of months after his death:

'The worst bit was showing the new people round. We had been so happy there but they were not a bit tactful and went through the rooms criticising everything – to hear them talk you would have thought it was a hovel but all my children had been born there and it was a place full of happy memories for me. It broke my heart hearing the house talked about in that way.'

The widow of a GP also lost her home:

'We lived in the practice house but when my husband died it was needed for the new doctor. His last illness had used up all our savings and there was not enough to buy another house outright. No building society would look at me either because I had no job and no qualifications. My husband had been self-employed and the NHS did not want to know about us. They reckoned he should have made his own pension arrangements while he was alive.

'There were four children at home and we moved from rented house to rented house like a family of gypsies. The houses were always too small for us and the children used to sleep on camp beds in the sitting-room. In fact the youngest ones loved that sort of life – it was like camping for them.

'We have our own house now with a room for everyone but for a bit of a lark the children will sometimes put up beds in the sitting-room and sleep there. I managed to buy a house after I qualified in my own profession and though it is not Buckingham Palace, I am tremendously proud of it. The house represents stability.'

Problems of homelessness can also affect widowers as well as widows. One man lived with his wife and son in a lodge cottage which was part of his wife's wage for doing domestic work in the large house to which it was attached. She died young of a brain haemorrhage and the husband and son had to move into rented accommodation nearby because his job as a farm labourer on another estate did not have a cottage with it. Another young man had worked as a prison officer but when his wife died, he found it impossible to work shift hours as well as looking after his two small children. Eventually he was forced to resign his job and of course lost his home as well.

Money played an all important part in the reminiscences of widowhood that came from men and women in all walks of life. Very few people said that they had no money worries, and one middle-aged widow who was left with a very generous company pension and a lump sum payment after her husband died had other dissatisfactions in her life. She has no children and was thrown into a life of aimless searching after interest and amusement.

'I've a splendid pension, but if I were to marry again it would be cut so I'm determined to go on living single until I'm eighty and draw every penny I can. Sometimes I think that I should take a job but I don't need the money and it would be very unfair to take work away from someone who really wants it. Voluntary work does not attract me because if there is no pressing reason to get up and go out in the morning, I am sure that I'd gradually lose interest. Many mornings, however, I lie in my bed and think that there is nothing at all I have to get up for.'

This was a very honest admission and I quote it not to make less well off people grind their teeth in disapproval but to show that even with money in your pocket, you have to be motivated to go on living. I often wonder if I would have done anything but mope and moan for the rest of my life if I had been left a rich widow. Would I have frittered away my time on foreign holidays and bridge afternoons? If I had I would have missed a great deal of amusement and interest because the fact that I have had to exercise my ingenuity to earn a living has completely transformed my life.

There was a time when if anyone asked what I did for a living, I could answer with complete honesty – 'I live on my wits.' That was when I was working as a freelance journalist and an adult education lecturer, plus being a landlady and running a holiday cottage letting business by remote control.

Landladying was the most profitable of those enterprises but without doubt it was the most fraught. Our house was large and rambling and when Adam died we were still in the process of having it modernized and decorated. He had been doing up the basement when he broke off to go on his last business trip to Singapore. It struck me that it could be rented out as a self-contained flat because it had a private door out into the garden and a tenant could live quite happily in its three rooms and bathroom. While I was still considering this project, fate sent me the perfect tenants, literally off the pavement. Sue, Anne and Denise had friends who were renting a similar basement in a house farther along the road. They were all students at Goldsmith's College and one evening there was a ring at my door and Sue stood there. She wanted to know if I had a basement flat that might be for rent.

That weekend the girls moved in and brought with them a feeling of youth and gaiety that seemed to permeate up through the floorboards of our rooms and lighten all our lives. I became as fond of the girls as if they were an extension of my family; they told me about their love affairs and when I was unhappy I talked to them. Their company and consideration was a very great help in tiding me over the worst first months after Adam died. I could weep in front of them without embarrassment and there is no greater sign of mutual regard and confidence than that.

### Children and Bereavement

The second problem of widowhood comes when there are children to consider.

There was no conscious calculation on my part to tell the children immediately about their father's death or to take the three eldest with me to his funeral – it merely seemed that their loss and grief must be as bad as mine and it was right that we should bear it together.

For a few minutes in the middle of the funeral service I was able to forget my own sorrow because my son, another Adam, who had been stoically dry-eyed and apparently unaffected since the day his father died, suddenly burst into tears and racking sobs. We stood side by side with my arm across his shaking little shoulders while he let loose the flood of his grief and it was then that I recognized the profound truth of the saying of Sophocles – 'children are the anchors that hold a mother to life'. My own misery was put into abeyance by Adam's distress.

The effect of death on my children taught me that it is misguided for a parent to believe that a child can survive the loss of a father or mother without deep emotional upset.

In Britain today there are over 200,000 children who have lost a parent to death and they will *all* experience trauma to a greater or lesser extent. To avoid the worst after-effects – the recurrent depressions, insecurities and even suicide attempts that have been the lot of bereaved children – it is essential for them to be able to understand what has happened. They must be allowed to grieve because when as adults they come to bad times in their lives, sorrow, anger and resentment is always increased by drawing on old hurts inflicted on them as children. If their reaction to parental death has never been fully worked out at the time, the later confusion is intensified. A parent who through sympathy tries to divert a child from grieving is laying up trouble for that child in the future. When I was researching this chapter I talked to many parents about what they told or would tell the children if the father or mother died. In spite of modern psychiatric awareness about the necessity to work through grief at any age, I was surprised how many people still advocate the mollifying approach.

'How can a child understand the concept of death?' asked one woman. 'Why should it be brought to their attention too early?'

In fact a child can understand death if it is presented to them in an understanding way. Tell children their parent has died, don't tell them he or she is 'broken' and has gone to God to be mended, as one mother said she told her daughter. The euphemisms used to avoid actually saying 'death' or 'died' can carry hidden terrors for the youngest children

Several parents said with confidence, 'My children came through the whole thing unaffected. They are so resilient. All that matters to them is to have one caring parent left to maintain the stability of their home. The big thing is not to interrupt their routine.'

This is the most condescending way of treating children – substitute the word 'dogs' for 'children' and you would have the same sort of people talking about their domestic pets.

Children find it much more difficult than adults to recognize and express grief. They are so confused about what has happened and why they feel as they do that they retreat into themselves looking to the adults around them for guidance as to how they are expected to behave. If a parent stoically puts on a brave front 'for the sake of the children' they have no mourning pattern to follow and the grief becomes repressed. A stone-faced widow or widower may think they are avoiding upsetting the children but the only result is to confuse them thoroughly. A child should see adults weeping and actively mourning in order to realize that they should not be ashamed of sorrow and tears.

Widowed parents should also talk to the children about the death and explain the circumstances. There have been several touching cases of children who, because adults always sheer off the reason why mummy or daddy died, subconsciously imagine that the child itself is in some way to blame. Perhaps the child has said or thought 'I wish you were dead' to the departed parent at some time – as everyone does when they are small and thwarted – and if the parent actually mysteriously disappears, the child can be emotionally scarred for life if reassurance is not given. Awareness has been growing for some years that children can be as deeply psychologically affected by a death in the family as a widow or widower and bereavement counselling services often accept sorrowing children as clients to help them work through the progress of grief.

Several parents, who had initially thought their children were 'taking it very well', told me how this impression was later disabused. A widow with two teenage daughters said, 'My girls were wonderful when my husband died. The eldest who had been very fond of her father was particularly unaffected – or so I thought. She hardly shed a tear, not even at his funeral. Our doctor asked me later how the girls were reacting and I said how well they were managing, especially the eldest. He looked at me very hard and said, "Don't you believe it. You'll have trouble there!" How right he was.'

The girl stayed calm for about a year and then became unmanageable, throwing tantrums round the house, being rude and defiant to her mother. The tension between them grew stronger until one day she suddenly burst out with: 'I hate you for staying alive when it was my father who died. I loved him best.'

Her mother, confused and saddened by this, said, 'I felt that if I were never to see her again it would be too soon.'

The unhappy girl left home and stayed away without communicating with her family for about a year. In the end however she returned, having rationalized her problems to herself. She has since settled down with her mother and sister and helps them run a family business.

Not all problem stories, however, end so happily. Another widow's daughter developed anorexia nervosa after her father died although when the death actually happened she did not seem to be suffering at all.

Her mother, weeping, explained the circumstances: 'Before his death my husband and I were contemplating divorce. We had even got to the stage of consulting a lawyer and our daughter knew about that. Then he was found to be suffering from cancer and died very quickly. I think my daughter imagined that his death pleased me and I could not convince her my grief was sincere. The mistake I made was putting a brave face on in the beginning because I thought it would be best for her if I tried to keep life going on much as usual.'

The girl refused to return to live with her mother after undergoing hospital treatment for anorexia. She stayed instead with her grandmother, still refusing to eat, and she died, aged nineteen, a few months before I met her mother.

Daughters, especially girls in their early teens, have a great attachment to their fathers and my own eldest daughter Pennie was typical. Before her father died she was working well at school in an effort to please him but afterwards she was transformed into a school drop-out and a troublesome rebel.

Because she wished to spare me anxiety, the school headmistress did not at first inform me of the deterioration in Pennie's behaviour and by the time I did get to know about it she was well embarked into a career of unruly rebellion, combining a complete lack of interest in her work with truancy. She seemed to be driven on by some kind of a demon, adding transgression to transgression to see how far she could go. At home her behaviour became impossible for she bullied the other children mercilessly and noisily and was sullen and uncommunicative to me. Attempts to remonstrate with her were met by a stony stare and an outburst: 'You're just jealous of me because I'm young and you're old and you haven't a man any more.'

Like the other mother whose daughter rounded on her, I was deeply hurt by this attack and our relationship deteriorated to a level of deep disapproval on my part and silent defiance on hers.

One afternoon she returned from a shopping trip with a friend and threw a bundle of packets of tights on the kitchen table. I asked where she got them because I knew she did not have enough money to buy them all.

'Shoplifted them, of course,' was the reply, thrown back over her shoulder as she stood making coffee at the cooker. The whole attitude was one of bravado – let's see what you do now.

'Take them back,' I said, gathering the packets together.
'What?'
'Take them back *now*.'
Amazingly, without any argument she gathered the packets

together and returned them to the Woolworth's store from which they had been taken. She later said that she felt more in danger replacing them on the counter than she had done when taking them. We talked about what had happened because at last we had reached the point where our problems had to be brought into the open. She said that throughout her bad time she had wanted me to act decisively, to do something to stop her and set some barriers around her so that she did not have to go so far that she would be entirely lost.

Of course there was no overnight reformation by my rebel daughter, though from then on she became more amenable at home. In school she continued to be in trouble until she left on the day she reached sixteen. Through her troubles there, however, our new understanding made it possible for me to stand up for her, and our relationship mended because she saw that I was not against her as everyone else seemed to be. Today she is a character of the greatest probity and I am very proud of her.

My other children showed a variety of reactions to Adam's death. Sarah, who is two years younger than Pennie, was deeply concerned about everyone else's grief and I remember driving the car with tears streaming down my cheeks and Sarah laying her arm along the seat back and cradling my neck with her hand. Textbooks say you should weep in front of your children and we were able to be sad together. As I write this Sarah is in India working at a centre for mentally disturbed children.

My son's reactions were much more complicated. I think boys have a conflict when they lose a father because in a way a male rival has been removed and they are set up, in their own minds at least, as head of a family. Adam, my husband, lost his own father when he was five years old. His father did not even live as long as his son did because he died in his late thirties. He worked in the coal mines, going to and fro from his job on a motor bike. One frosty morning, he had an accident on the bike and came home early saying he felt unwell. He went to bed in one of the old-fashioned box beds in the kitchen which were a common feature in Scottish working-class homes at that time. His youngest child, Adam, who was off school because of a cold, was tucked in beside his father. He told me what happened.

'I remember my mother coming over to bring my father a cup of tea. She shook him by the shoulder and then started to cry – he was dead.'

The fact that his father had died had been completely unnoticed by the sleeping child at his side. The official cause of death on Adam's father's death certificate was a perforated ulcer but there was no autopsy and the local doctor who was called in only filled in the form as best he could. Now it seems as if the death must have been some sort of cardiac failure – perhaps he passed his frailty on to his son.

Surprisingly Adam carried no traumatic memories of that terrifying afternoon into his life and he was always able to talk about it with detachment. I remember him once discussing with another man who was also made fatherless very young, what advantages they felt that not having a father had brought them. They were both quite convinced that losing a father had been more formative than destructive. The friend was a very successful self-made man and he declared that his later business career was made possible because he had been given confidence and self-reliance after his father died.

'I never had any rival,' he explained.

I could see this attitude developing in my son too and it was always a shock to his sisters and me when he came out with pronouncements of great chauvinism. 'How can you say that?' we would shout in horror. 'After all, you have been brought up in a household of women.' Perhaps he could be a chauvinist precisely because of that.

Young Adam's reactions to his father's death were less easy to pinpoint and understand than his sisters' because they seemed to have been compounded by a feeling of freedom and genuine grief. This confusion expressed itself in anger. His sisters remember that when I left the room after telling them that Adam senior had died, their brother's reaction was terrifying.

'He began to scream and scream,' said Sarah. 'I was really frightened because I don't think I have ever seen anyone in such a terrible rage. He was furious, really furious.'

That was, however, his only outburst until the day of the funeral when his sorrow was quieter and more restrained. After that he settled down, apparently little affected, and his only obvious reaction to what happened has been total disillusion with religion. Quite soon after Adam's death, our son told me: 'I don't believe in any God. I don't think He exists. If He did how could our father just die like that?'

He has always refused to go to church with us even when there was a carol service or on the red letter day when Eleanor was picked to read the lesson in our village church. It seemed as if a church boycott was part of his defiance of any deity.

Another widow, who had a son aged seven when his father died, was also surprised by the anger and violence of his early reactions.

'One night just after my husband died, I was putting my son to bed and he suddenly began kicking and screaming like a wild thing. He kept shouting "I want him back, I want him back" and there was nothing I could do to quieten him. His rage was an expression of his inability to understand why someone he loved so much had been taken from him.'

The reactions of my youngest child Eleanor showed me that it is a mistake to imagine that even very young children are not affected by the death of a parent. She was just over two when her father died and I thought that she could have little concept of what was happening. Her father had spent a lot of time away from home on business trips and it seemed to me that he had not played a very dominant role in Eleanor's life. When we all went to the funeral she was left at home with friends and a few months later, when another friend invited us to go to Cyprus for a holiday, again Eleanor was left behind.

On our return however I found that I had misjudged the awareness and deep feelings of a two-year-old, because my friend told me that Eleanor had wept constantly for the two weeks of our holiday and had spent her time sitting forlornly in the sitting-room window watching the road for our reappearance. She was afraid that we might have all disappeared as arbitrarily as her father had done. When she saw me however she turned away and would not talk to me for she was angry at my betrayal and abandonment of her.

To this day she is terrified of being lost or cut off from the rest of the family. Shopping in a big store means that Eleanor is almost hanging on to my skirt. Though she now feels too adult to hold her mother's hand, she sticks so close to me that very often she treads down the backs of my shoes and if I wander off without her, she goes red in the face and hisses indignantly, 'Don't go off and leave me.'

Helping children recover from the death of a parent means you have to be very sensitive to their needs and confusion. Sympathy and understanding is always lavished on the widow or widower, not on the children who need it just as much. The saddest case I came across while researching this chapter was that of a widow with a teenage son who had been born six months after his father was killed in an accident. This happened in the Far East where they were then living and the young woman returned to live with her mother. The baby was born in the same local hospital as she had been born in herself. While he was growing up the child was never given any insight into his father's life, there were no links at all with the shadowy, little-talked-of man who had conceived him. It was almost deliberate policy on the mother's part to shut the son out of that part of her life; she kept the memory of her husband to herself like a private possession which could not be shared. Any affection she extended to the boy was grudging and both he and she felt he had been a drain on her resources and a tether to her life. Talking about the strained situation that had developed between them by the time he was fifteen, she said, 'I was not in a fit state to have a baby after my husband died. There have been many times that I would rather have the father back than the child.'

Of course the boy was aware of his mother's feelings. In fact many children are afraid that their surviving parent would rather have lost them than the person who died and they need constant reassurance that the love felt for them is undiminished and is not some sort of barter love. Allowing them to share in adult grief is an understanding way to do this because it allows them to see that they are considered to be in an equally suffering position to the mourning adult – they are party to a great confidence.

Much has been written about the problems of bringing up children on your own. What should also be pointed out, however, is that the bringing up of children is one of the most satisfying things that any human being can do – whether alone or in partnership. Children are our biggest investment in the future, they are our continuing lives. It is possible to bring up a family alone and, like widowhood itself, there are often consolations to be found in the fact that you are the only person at the head of a family. You have no divided loyalties, no conflicting emotions. There is no one else to play off the children against you or for them to use as a weapon in the parents versus children war. Many possible areas of conflict are removed for the one parent family. Recently I was listening to a radio discussion on this subject and after a long recital of woes and worries, a woman rang in to say that she had brought up two sons on her own and 'I'd like people to know it *can* be done,' she said. 'Now my sons are both grown up and successful and it is very satisfying for me to look back and see what I have accomplished. Of course we had our worries and we went through bad times but there were wonderful times as well and in the end everything has been worthwhile.'

That for me was the most constructive contribution to the whole programme. Don't whine, don't look back in bitterness to what you once had and might have had if death had been more considerate. Concentrate instead on the life enhancing things about having children and bringing them up. Of course you will have worries – about money, about children's health, about their opportunities and jobs or lack of them – but even families with two parents have those worries.

One of my saddest days as a parent on my own was the afternoon when my youngest daughter came home from nursery school and innocently asked me, 'What is it like to have a daddy?'

Another little girl in her class had been taunting her about having no father. I was angry until I remembered the line by Elizabeth Bowen in *The Death of the Heart* about there being no limit to the violations that children inflict on each other. The only way I could answer Eleanor's question was to build a mental image of her father for her and I took care to tell her stories about him, relating particular incidents that had taken place after she was born and always telling her where she was and what she was doing when they took place. I told her how much he had loved her, how thrilled he was when he came to the hospital to see her lying in her cot and how he then rushed out to buy the teddy bear which she took to bed with her every night. I told her how he would always ask 'How's the baby?' first when he rang us up from his foreign trips. The older children too told stories, the family folklore that every family has. We would sit in the evening and laugh about funny things that had happened, because Adam senior had been a very funny man, and bit by bit Eleanor was able to build a memory of her father, an idealized one perhaps, but he became a flesh and blood character for her instead of a shadowy ghost. When she went to boarding school last summer I found a photograph of him with her on his knee which she took so that she could look at it and have a true idea of what it is like 'to have a daddy'.

Another problem that worried me was that my son was growing up in a household of women. For the first few months after Adam died, we had one or two offers from the husbands of friends to include Adam in expeditions with their sons but bit by bit those offers stopped – people forgot about us, so there was no regularity or pattern to his masculine outings.

It had been my husband's wish for his son to go to boarding school. During the last year of his life we made desultory efforts to find a prep school for Adam and visited several establishments where long concrete corridors, sweaty socks and muddy boots in the cloakrooms and the smell of overcooked food in the air totally repelled me. It was not the sort of life I wanted for my son and when Adam was alive I was determined to gradually divert him away from the boarding school idea. Unfortunately when he died, I had a fit of misguided loyalty and thought it would be best to follow his plans for our son. When Adam was nine he was to go to a school which his father had selected as being the most suitable. His rule of thumb had been to pick one that produced the most Scottish rugby internationalists. He was fanatically keen on rugby, had played himself and wanted his son to do the same. In fact when Adam was born his father's present to him had been a miniature rugby ball which he laid in the cot beside the baby. When I protested – for the rugby club ethic never appealed to me – he said with total conviction – 'But he has to learn to handle it and the sooner the better.'

The men who were in charge of our trust fund thought my decision to send Adam to school was a sign that I was going to turn out to be a model widow. They agreed to pay the fees out of our capital. 'He needs a male environment,' they all agreed. How wrong we were. The school was a complete disaster as far as Adam was concerned. I was shattered to receive letters from him spattered with tear marks and saying – 'I hate it here. Please take me home.' I should have done just that but I steeled my heart instead and everyone assured me that this was the right thing to do – 'They all try it on at first,' I was told. Adam never did settle down however and he hated the school till the day I finally withdrew him. He never fitted in with its hearty male chauvinism. When he left, he was sent to a South London comprehensive where he was very much happier and more extended in every way. His work that had been abysmally bad at boarding school began to show signs of improvement and he made many friends.

The anxieties of finding male companionship for fatherless sons are shared by many widows and they are often advised to introduce male companions into their homes – but what they are not told is how this can be done. Many widows live lonely, isolated existences far away from their own male relatives and the nature of widowhood is such that male companionship is automatically cut off from them. Moreover the presence of children is often an inhibiting factor for women trying to re-establish contact with men. One widower interviewed for this book said that when he met a woman with children he did not pursue the acquaintance – 'I clear off if they have kids. No way am I going to be saddled with another man's children.' His attitude is far from rare.

In America there is a 'Big Brother' organization which is an effort to solve the problem of mothers with fatherless sons. Boys can go for outings or even for holidays with host families where there are two parents. The host family are volunteers – no payment is made except for the usual pocket money which a mother would give her son in any case or the payment of accommodation if he accompanies the 'Big Brother' family on holiday. The families are able to get together and meet each other before the arrangements are finalized.

In Sussex there was an organization called Singlehanded which puts fatherless or motherless families in contact with each other to share either social outings and holidays or living accommodation. This was different from the 'Big Brother' idea because it was meant to provide more permanent arrangements but it was often a solution for many problems.

Apart from the practicalities of life however there can be other problems for the children and remaining parent of a widowed family. Too often the death burdens the child or children with responsibilities beyond their years . . . 'I worry about you,' is a frequent cry from children to a parent whose partner has died. The loss of a mother can often be the most upsetting for children's lives. One family interviewed were left motherless when the three children were thirteen, five and two. The father of the family was a working man who could not afford to pay for a full-time housekeeper and for a short time they relied on the good offices of neighbours but those eventually stopped.

Before a year had passed the eldest child of the family had the responsibilities of a mother thrust upon her. At an age when her contemporaries were going to parties and playing games with friends, she was emotionally and physically tied to her younger brother and sister – cooking for them, taking them to school, staying at home to look after them when they were sick. In her early twenties now, she is still in charge of the little family. Surprisingly she has no bitterness about the loss of her own childhood, only a certain wistful longing for the opportunities she has missed.

'I often think it would be nice to get away from this small town and see the world. I was once offered a job in the city but I knew I could not take it. There would be no one to look after the little ones. If I packed my suitcase to leave, I'd be repacking it next day to come back again. They could never manage without me. Last year I went with some friends to Majorca for a fortnight and it was the first time I had been away. The whole time I was worried about what was happening at home and I had to phone them every night to see if they were all right.'

Her maternal attitude also extends to her father who she describes as 'a bit of a muddler'. She recalled what happened when her mother died:

'I knew my mother was ill but it never struck me that she might die. The doctors in the hospital never mentioned the possibility and I think it even took my father by surprise – more because he refused to consider the possibility than anything else. In the beginning I took on all the arrangements for the funeral, the flowers and the tea and all the things like that. It was at least a month before the full shock of her death really hit me and then I knew that it was up to me to take on her job.'

Her father is aware of the sacrifices his daughter has had to make. He said, 'But we had no alternative. People offered to help at first but it didn't last long, we had to get on with it on our own. I know my daughter has had a raw deal but there was little I could do about it.'

Even in less dramatic circumstances children can be left confused and unhappy by parental death. Even in such a simple thing as not being able to understand why a mother who was once a generous spender should suddenly become penny-pinching. It is essential always to explain the situation to children even though they may not seem old enough to appreciate the nuances of the argument – they realize a great deal more than they are given credit for realizing.

In Britain today there are more than one and a quarter million dependent children living in one parent families. This figure includes the children of divorced and separated parents and those whose parents were never married. There are also a large number of children who spend some time in one parent families but whose parents later remarry. No matter what the circumstances, those children have a great many problems in common and over the last decade awareness of those problems and efforts to solve them have been growing. There are now several organizations that can offer help and advice to people bringing up children on their own and in the last chapter there is a list of names and addresses that might prove useful. One of the most interesting of the organizations is Gingerbread whose success is proof of what can be done by a group of people with the same problems getting together to solve them. There is no area of one parent family life that Gingerbread cannot advise on and recently they set up their first child day care centre in Croydon – Gingerbread Corner, which can cater for over one hundred children. If the idea were adopted in other parts of the country it could be the answer to a prayer for thousands of working parents.

Bereaved parents should never blind themselves to the needs of their children but they should remember that a family can hold together with love and that togetherness can assuage some of the agonies of mourning. Bringing up a family on your own is a triumph of love.

**Touching People is Good**

"I just popped in to our
neighbourhood sex shop on
my way home from church."

The third and often the most pressing and permanent problem
of widowhood is the unsatisfied need for sex and companionship.

The most anguished cry of the widowed is 'I'm so lonely'
for loneliness and the need for love is at the root of the most

fraught reactions. Saying 'I'm lonely' also may mean that you are sexually frustrated, lonely for the touch of another person's hand and for the reassurance that somewhere in the world there is one other person to whom you are all important and who is of overwhelming importance to you.

Margaret Hamilton, who married the abrasive MP after they had both been widowed, described her unhappiness in widowhood as 'I felt as if I had suddenly been shut out of the world.' When she married again she said, 'It is like a fairy tale. I feel as if I have come in from the cold.'

Many widowed people are reluctant to admit even to themselves the true reason for their continuing desolation and women in particular prefer to give their misery the socially acceptable icing of sanctified mourning. They never admit to missing sex but say they long for 'that big hug' or, more vaguely, 'companionship'. To admit to being sexually deprived seems like an admission of defeat to them.

Often in an effort to find a focus for their sadness, they live in the past, their conversation always begins with 'I had' and they deliberately close their eyes to any good things that their present might contain. With the 'I had' life often goes an almost unrealistic memory of the dead wife or husband. Everyone knows mourning widows who set up their dead husbands like household gods, peerless paragons of men.

Two very unhappy widows who talked about their reasons for being so desolate said, 'When God made my husband He broke the mould' and 'I never met his like when he was alive and I'm unlikely to do so now that he is dead.'

This, they feel, justifies their frustrations for like acolytes they have dedicated themselves to a memory. Much as I respect their loyalty it is necessary to point out that their logic is completely at fault.

An extreme case of the dedicated widow was a woman who was not unhappy but positively radiant with memories of the dead paragon husband whom she brought into the conversation continually, enthusiastically extolling his virtues. He seemed too good to be true and her placidity at the fact of losing such a saint seemed surprising – until a mutual acquaintance asked if I had been hearing the dead husband stories. I said he seemed like a man in a million and the other woman laughed.

'He was a mean devil,' came the snorted reply. 'She was simply terrified of him when he was alive – he never let her go out on her own and grudged her money for clothes and food. She is a changed woman since he went, her life has begun really, but she cannot bring herself to admit she is glad he is dead and puts up this false image of him.'

The last time I saw the joyous widow she told me about her husband's last illness and his last words. She said that they were very significant of his care for her.

'He was in hospital and I was sitting by the bed. He was taken ill just before we were booked to go on a coach tour of the Highlands and he was so thoughtful of me that his very last words were – "Don't forget to claim the Wallace Arnold refund" . . . don't you think that showed how much he was looking after me even with his last breath?'

What that widow was unable to admit was that she would not want her husband back. A more ordinary reaction is a sense of deep deprivation and longing which carries with it a hope of remarriage or at least of finding a new lover. But the chances of widowed women remarrying are slight. To face cold statistics drives romantic hopes away.

The overall figure for widows of any age remarrying in Britain is only 3 per cent and the figure for widows in Britain has remained fairly constant over the last ten years at around three million. That means that only around 90,000 of those has any chance of remarrying. In Britain one woman in six is a widow. In the USA, allowing for divorce and separation as well as for women who have never married, 37 per cent of the female population live without a man.

A look at the graphs for the ages of widowhood is also fairly depressing – in Great Britain, according to figures provided by the Office of Population Statistics and Survey, only 1700 of the female population are widowed under the age of 24 but for every ten-year age gap thereafter the figure climbs steadily – 11,500 up to age 34; 172,800 between 45 and 54; 315,100 up to the age of 64 and 1,366,000 for women over 75.

The comparative graph for widowers shows how many more women are left bereaved than men – the figure for men who are widowed under 24 is 300; between 45 and 54 the figure is 42,700; by the age of 64 the figure climbs to 72,200 – less than a quarter of the number of widows at the same age and by 75 plus there are 315,500 widowers.

It has been estimated that at no matter the age she is when widowed the average British woman in that position can look forward to fifteen years on her own. In America, the widow can look forward to ten years of solitary living. It seems a long time to waste yearning for the return of something you are unlikely to find.

The position for widowers is very different. Middle-aged men who lose their wives have a remarriage rate of over 87 per cent and the average length of time that a man can expect to remain alone is just over eight months. Eight months or fifteen years – it is a vast differential. Widowed men are also not bound by the same age strictures when they look for a new partner and it is not considered outrageous for a widower to marry a woman very much his junior. A woman who did that – and the chances of it are even more statistically remote than of remarriage at all – would be considered foolishly optimistic and self-deceiving.

Many women are made angry and resentful when they consider the vast differences between a sentence of widowhood for men and themselves. Resentment, however, does nothing to solve the problem – a better solution is to find resources within oneself and to devise some other way of life than conventional marriage which will bring as much satisfaction as possible. The first decision that must be made is sorting out your own priorities.

I once knew a woman so immaculate and painstaking that she ironed her tights before putting them on. When she told me about that part of her routine I felt as if she had handed me the key to her personality. Morning callers always found her in full make-up – even to the false eyelashes – doing her chores in a pretty frilly apron 'because you never know who is going to turn up'. She believed that life is a sort of campaign in which you must first define your objectives and then lay your plans about how to achieve them.

As far as she was concerned it was insupportable for a woman to live without a man. She had been married three times and was the gallant survivor of one widowing and a divorce when I met her. She chose her husbands for financial support, security and sex and her side of the bargain was to present herself in the best light at all times and to run their homes with clockwork efficiency. Sex was a very big priority as far as she was concerned – 'Intercourse is the best thing for the complexion,' she said, proffering a satin smooth cheek for my inspection.

After Adam died she was very kind to me and invited me to dinner on several occasions to meet 'eligible' men but in the end she grew impatient with me as a pupil because I was completely unable to organize myself in what she regarded as a premier area of life – I failed to find myself another husband.

That lady shared a lot of the ideas of the Roman emperor Augustus who had no time for the idea of a sad widow romantically devoted to the memory of her husband. He ruled that all widows between the ages of twenty-five and fifty should remarry within a year or be penalized. The length of time for mourning was later extended to two years but the firm commitment to remarriage remained.

My thrice married friend tried to instruct me in the best husband hunting tactics.

'Always be on the lookout for a suitable man. One way is to read the obituary columns in case anyone you know dies. I met my last husband that way for I knew him and his wife slightly and one day I saw that she had died. I wrote a letter of sympathy saying I understood how he felt because I had been a widow myself. Then I popped along to see how he was getting on and we were married three months later.'

It was practical and expedient for them both but it worked out very well. Another widow was looking for much the same arrangement when she told me, 'I'd marry anyone, simply anyone just to have a man in my life again.'

Were those ladies businessmen they would probably end up as captains of industry, but for my own part I find it impossible to follow their rules – not only am I constitutionally incapable of ironing my tights but I find it difficult at times to remember to put them on.

I suspect that the majority of widows are more like me than like the organized ladies and for us it seems there is little option other than the advice that Hamlet gave Ophelia, 'Get thee to a nunnery'.

This is hard advice for women to accept especially if they are still young and vigorous. They can hardly react other than with repressed rage against their exclusion from what they had expected in life. One woman said sadly, 'When you have been doing something for years and think you are rather good at it, it is hard to reconcile yourself to the idea that it is gone forever. I wish there was either some way of reconciling myself to living without sex or, even better, of providing myself with it now that I am a widow.'

She said that one of her strongest longings was to touch other people and she pointed out a passage in a novel by Ed McBain called *Vanishing Ladies* which graphically described this human need.

'It's like a big taboo . . . this taboo says "Don't touch". Marriage makes touching alright. When you are married you get to be one person. You got no secrets anyway. You belch, you yell, you spill things on the dinner table – in other words you share with another person the secret that you are only an animal with a mind. But that's where the taboo is lifted and nowhere else.'

It may not be great literature but it says everything that widows and widowers feel about the frustration of being alone.

For sexual frustration is not peculiar to women. Men suffer from it too but they are more open to admitting their needs –

such an admission is not considered unseemly in a man. A widower talking about his frustrations ten years after his wife died said, 'If a man tells you he never desires a woman when he is widowed he is telling you a lie. For even when you are happily married it is normal to indulge your imagination in a bit of wishful thinking from time to time. For me that was only ever a flight of fancy but when my wife died, the fancying became a pressing reality.'

The trouble for him was that he and his wife had been sole sexual partners since their late teens and he was held back from forming another association because of his fear that he would call the new woman by his wife's name.

'My main fear was that in a moment of passion and forgetfulness I might call some other woman "Mary". I avoided chances to sleep with people because I was so afraid of that happening. It would not only have been a betrayal of my wife but an insult to the new woman. It took me years to overcome my dread and I only conquered it recently when I met a woman who I know will understand if I call her "Mary" by mistake.'

People condemned to unwilling chastity live in a half world of hope. In their nunnery they are cheered from time to time by the news from the outside world of some widow or widower remarrying and that gives a lift to the spirits – perhaps it *is* possible after all. Mrs Willie Hamilton received a great many letters of congratulation from people she had never met when she remarried at the age of sixty-three because her story seemed the embodiment of so many dreams.

It is, however, a pity for people to live their lives in a half world of romantic imagining. Recently I was at the wedding of a spinster in her late forties who suddenly surprised everyone by getting married. One of the telegrams read out at the reception said 'You can stop reading Barbara Cartland now' and I thought it very cruel. As well as living vicariously in love stories, many widows can make themselves unhappy by weaving love plots in their own minds with themselves as the heroine. They develop adolescent crushes on some man of their acquaintance and can convince themselves that their affection is returned. Some very unhappy situations have arisen this way.

More practical people recognize their need for human companionship and set up home with another woman. Occasionally those are lesbian arrangements but more frequently they are the coming together of two people who need each other's company. It is interesting to observe that after a period of time, two women living together will take on male/female roles in the menage. One does the fixing of the plugs and taking the car to bits; the other cooks and mends the clothes. For sexual outlet a lot of women are driven to masturbation but this is something to which few will openly admit and one woman who said that she masturbated gave it up after a while because it only exacerbated her longing for a lover – 'It made everything worse. I found it was better to have no satisfaction at all. It was easier to live that way.'

That same woman was made angry and upset by the amount of pro-sex advertising that she saw around her.

'We are bombarded by it,' she said. 'On television there are explicit love scenes, in the bookshops there are shelves of magazines telling people how to make love. It makes me really sad because I know how to do it and it seems that I'm never going to get another chance.'

The Christian religion has always given a high place to the ideal of celibacy – it is made to appear in some ways preferable to marriage – 'Better to marry than to burn'. The ideal of chastity has connotations of ceremonial purity. Today, however, people are more aware of the unnatural repressions that enforced chastity brings and the popular view of the celibate has swung in the opposite direction. Now it is very unfashionable for anyone to admit to chastity because they are then thought of as being unnaturally repressed and in some way guilty of denying their natural appetites. This thoroughgoing disapproval of chastity is, however, just as misguided as the high-minded prudery that went before, and some balance has to be struck between accepting the need to be open about our sexual drives and the respect that is due to people who choose not to or are unable to give sex a predominant role in their lives.

The most successful way to live as a celibate is to replace the need for love with another outlet. The German pastor Dietrich Bonhoeffer wrote that the essence of chastity was 'the total orientation of one's life towards a goal'. The goal, whether it is for enlightenment or success, towards helping others or improving and helping yourself, becomes the substitute for sexual love.

The recipe that is most likely to succeed is work. If I have ever to try to help other lonely people with advice I hear myself saying 'You ought to get a job.' It makes me feel like Mrs Smiling, a character in Stella Gibbons's wonderfully funny book *Cold Comfort Farm*. Mrs Smiling's answer for all life's problems was 'Get a job' and when Flora, the heroine, did not do as she was told, Mrs Smiling exhorted her 'Flora, don't be FEEBLE' . . . My recipe is 'Don't be FEEBLE, widows, find a job and forget your other hang-ups.'

Recently there was an extremely interesting interview with Diana Trilling, wife of the writer Lionel Trilling, in the *International Herald Tribune* which summed up everything that I feel myself about widowhood. She said that she missed her husband sorely when he died: ·

'You know the genius who invented marriage was inventing an extraordinary institution in which each of the two people is the most important person in the world to the other and this is something the closest friendship cannot provide. Doing work that satisfies you is the nearest thing to reassurance of that kind. I don't want to make myself out to be a lamentable case, because I'm not. I have a professional career. I have a place in the world. I'm very fortunate.

'Widowhood nonetheless is hell. Of course it's lonely and the only antidote I know to loneliness is work, really. People are not an antidote, they often increase the loneliness.'

Everyone can think of numerous cases of people finding a satisfying sublimation in work. Field Marshal Montgomery was a dedicated celibate after his wife died.

There are many other less celebrated examples – a widow in her forties went to law school and qualified as a solicitor when her husband died. Another woman, interviewed for this book, was the head of a thriving business which she took over when it was very ailing at the time of her husband's death.

She said, 'My only contact with the company had been doing the odd bit of typing for my husband if his secretary was off. When he died I was determined it was not going to be sold or closed down because he had given his life for it. The worry about its shaky state had brought on his coronary, and I did not want that sacrifice to be for nothing.

'For ten days after his funeral I kept his business briefcase full of papers at the side of my bed but I did not have the courage to open it. Then one morning, at 4 a.m., I got up and started. The sweat was pouring off me. Everything was even worse than I had suspected – the business was in a terrible state but the realization of that galvanized me.'

After three years of hard work she is the head of a thriving company, accepted as boss by her workforce and proud of her ability to run the concern.

'It gives me a thrill when a customer walks in and heads straight for me as if he knows that I'm the boss. I used to see people doing that with my husband and I wondered how they were always able to pick him out. Now they do it with me.'

She is very aware that her dedication to work has been her substitute for sex.

'I used to be fairly highly sexed but while I've been so busy I haven't given it a thought. Now the business is getting on a good footing I'm more discontented. I'll either have to find myself another man or start another business.'

A widower also described how he gave himself the twin aims of becoming successful in his career and raising his children when his wife died.

'The lack of a woman did not bother me a lot at first because I was so busy. When I considered marrying again I remembered some people I had known when I was young; they had a stepmother who was very cruel to them and I did not want to run the risk of the same thing happening to my children. Now the children are grown up and I have a very good professional career and from time to time I think I may have made a mistake in not remarrying but it seems too late now. No one would take me on at this stage.'

His disclaimer 'no one would take me on' is a clue to another of the causes of the feelings of inadequacy and un-happiness in widowhood. Women in particular are plagued by those because they are often widowed when their first youth and attractiveness is past. They have wrinkles and grey hair and no one in the world to tell them they are loved. It is difficult not to feel unworthy of esteem if there is no one to bolster your confidence by the ever consoling knowledge of their long-established love and regard for you – in spite of the middle age spread. When you forget what it was like to be loved, you also experience a massive loss of self-confidence.

But it is not necessary to fall into a pit of self-distaste and insecurity for women in their middle age have many things to be proud of – a breadth of knowledge, a philosophy and tolerance that comes with experience. Because they are dif-ferent from the young women they were when they entered the sexual arena for the first time, they are battling for differ-ent goals. Many women say that if they married again, they would be looking for a different type of man from their first husbands.

The marriages and liaisons of older people often have a greater degree of success and stability than those in the younger age groups. People with an awareness of their own value and a firm grip of their own opinions have also learned to look on life with a leavening of tolerance and humour.

If the life of working chastity is found insufficient, people who are determined to change their situation nearly always manage to do so. It is only when you are half-hearted or inhibited by feelings of your own inability to succeed that you miss your aim.

Many men and women have to overcome their secret fears of their sexual ignorance before they can embark on the great search for another partner. Even in the ostensibly liberated 1980s it is surprising how many people have only had experience of one partner. The dread of revealing this holds many people back from embarking on a new association.

A widow said, 'I had only slept with one man in my life – my husband. I could not imagine what it would be like with anyone else. I had never been a flirtatious sort of woman either and had no idea how to go about finding myself another lover. By great good luck one found *me* and the first time I was in bed with him, I found to my vast relief that his story was the same as mine – he had only ever slept with one woman, his wife.'

Sometimes the solution of finding a new partner is also inhibited by a feeling that you are guilty of infidelity to the dead husband or wife. The woman whose new lover found her said that though her husband had been dead for several years by that time, she was haunted by the feeling that she was committing adultery. 'If my husband had come storming through the door and found us in bed,' she said, 'I would not have been surprised.'

Men too suffer from hidden feelings of guilt about making new associations after a wife dies. One widower was apparently very satisfied with his life and said that he always has liaisons with an average of four women at a time – 'I'm not deceiving any one of them, they all know about each other. I go out with one when I'm in a certain mood and with another when I need something else. They all satisfy various aspects of my personality or my interests. I have no intention of marrying any one of them.'

Talking about his initial reactions to his wife's death, he said, 'It shattered me. I was completely grief-ridden for about four months. She died in November and I was back in bed again – if you know what I mean – in May and after that I was fine. I have never looked back since.'

He was not a man given to circumlocution and the unnaturally coy phrase 'back in bed again' was significant of the unease he felt about his resumption of a sex life. He also still hallucinated about seeing his wife though she had been dead for almost ten years.

'I often wake up in the morning and there she is sitting on the end of my bed. The vision only lasts for seconds but it is very vivid and it always seems as if we have been talking about some current concern of mine.'

He added, 'It doesn't happen a lot now, just every so often but it is always worst around the anniversary of her death.'

The same man said that he kept a selection of his wife's clothes and from time to time loaned a stole or a handbag to one of his lady friends – but always insisted on getting it back. Somehow there was nothing romantic about those revelations and I mentioned the case to a psychotherapist who worked a great deal with widowed people. He said that though hallucinations of the person who has died are very common among the newly bereaved, they gradually wear off. For them to persist for ten years was unusual and he suggested that the widower might be in fact very guilty about his vigorous sex life and that it might also be an act of defiance against women in general and his wife in particular.

'I think it sounds as if she was the dominant member of the marriage who called the tune in their relationship. His feelings could be a combination of guilt and rebellion,' said the psychotherapist.

Guilty or not it is much easier for a man to re-establish contact with the opposite sex than it is for a woman. A young widower was astonished and delighted at the reception he had from available women:

'I couldn't believe the number of offers that were made to me, mainly from married women who were bored with their husbands and looking for adventure with no strings attached. I am a heterosexual with a capital H and it was like manna from heaven. I think they were sorry for me in a way and also they felt safe at making a pass at a widower – they knew I wasn't a homosexual and was not likely to turn them down.'

It was observing situations like this that made a widow say rather bitterly, 'I wish I was an honorary man. My need for sex is as strong as any man's but I'm not able to admit it or to do anything positive about it. Society and my own conventionality hold me back. If I go into a bar alone everyone thinks I'm there to pick up a man. Sleazy characters think I'm open to any approach. I'm not permitted to pick and choose. If a man goes looking for another woman everyone says "poor thing" and assumes he is blameless and lonely. It is not considered natural for a woman to do the same thing.'

Even women who are liberated from the more stringent strictures and old attitudes are also bound by the assumption that men do the pursuing and women should sit still and wait to be asked.

'I don't think men and women can ever be regarded as truly equal until a woman has the freedom to say "Let's go to bed" to a man she fancies,' said a single woman, who is to every appearance very liberated. 'Younger people are coming to accept this but older women would rather bite their nails in frustration than make the first approach. I have made a career for myself in a man's world and know that I should be able to organize my sex life just as efficiently as I organize everything else – but I can't. From time to time I've been the one to ask the question but it is always to someone who I know is not going to turn me down. I couldn't take a chance on the answer being "No, thanks". My definition of a gentleman is one who takes "No" for an answer but I don't know if I would be capable of acting like a gentlewoman in those circumstances.'

Women are also acutely conscious that no matter how frustrated and deprived of love they are, they need to feel some affection and respect for the men with whom they sleep. One of the wails of widows is about being approached by predatory men – 'It is always the ones I don't want who make passes at me,' said one woman.

The majority of those approaches, surprisingly, come from the husbands of friends and acquaintances. A doctor who counsels the bereaved also said that many widows were distressed by having sexual approaches made to them by professional advisers.

'I was really surprised when I found out how many women are propositioned by men like lawyers, bank managers and other financial advisers. The line taken is usually "I've helped you so why don't you do this for me?" Several of the women who told me about their experiences were deeply distressed and embarrassed by what had happened.'

A more common experience is for widows to find themselves approached by the husbands of friends.

'I was really hurt when I was first widowed to realize that as far as some of my women friends were concerned, I suddenly became an object of suspicion and was dropped. They would invite me to morning coffee or afternoon tea but I was strictly kept away from gatherings where there would be men. They all seemed to think that I was on a scalp-hunting expedition and the women who were the most worried were the ones whose husbands I would not have touched with a barge pole. But I soon began to realize that they had grounds for their anxieties because husbands do make passes at women on their own.

'One afternoon about six weeks after my husband's funeral, the husband of a neighbour turned up at my door. I had no idea what he wanted but I invited him in and offered him a cup of tea. While we were sitting making awkward conversation, he suddenly jumped up, rubbed his hands together and said:

'"Well, let's get on with it before your kids come back from school."

'I stared at him: "Get on with what?"

'"Going to bed, of course," was his answer. He was as cold and clinical as that. I was furious. I shouted and yelled and ordered him out of the house. When he left he said, "I thought you'd be needing it by now." He seemed to think there was something wrong with me for turning his offer down. After he left I wept because I was in a strange way ashamed of what had happened – I felt as if it was my fault in a way and I felt unclean. There seems to be a popular male myth that a widow is ripe for taking – by anybody.'

That woman's unwanted suitor also turned out to be a revengeful liar and took his revenge on her by telling his wife that she had made a pass at him. The widow was dropped by her old circle of friends and she could not understand what was wrong until, several months later, the story leaked back to her. Even when she attempted to put the record straight, there were several people who still distrusted her on the old 'no smoke without fire' theory.

Widows stand in very real danger of losing their reputation. A man said, 'Men who lose their wives are expected to find a bit on the side very quickly and if they don't some people think they are unnatural. But even in fairly large communities a woman has to watch her reputation and it is difficult if not impossible to hide what she is doing. Talk gets round. Sometimes a woman can lose her good name innocently and without realizing it. I have myself been in male company with one man boasting about his conquests and naming names. The men all round him laugh away even though some of them suspect the stories are not true. Very often the stories are lies and wishful thinking but there's nothing the woman involved can do about it.'

One of the saddest aspects of widowhood is how vulnerable women become to unscrupulous men and their own romantic longings. Every promise means faith and permanency to them and often they put up with all sorts of unreasonable behaviour just to have a man back in their lives again. After I wrote an article about widowhood in a woman's magazine I received a spate of letters and one of the most upsetting was from a widow in her fifties who wrote that she had been alone for several years and had brought up two daughters when suddenly 'one of my deepest held wishes came true'. She met a man of thirty-two who became her lover.

She wrote, 'I really believed it when he said that he loved me and that we had a future together. Our sex life was ecstatic and I had never known anything like it, even in my years of marriage. Then after only three months he has stopped seeing me and I am left worse off than I was before. He has aroused feelings and desires that can't be turned off. I nearly go mad with frustration, screaming and banging my head against the wall. It is taking tremendous will power to pull myself back to life and I know now that I must be very wary of committing myself again.'

The desolation of loneliness makes every widow or widower susceptible to a bit of wishful thinking now and again and sometimes it becomes so pressing that they join dating agencies, marriage bureaux or singles' clubs in the hope of finding a compatible partner. It is difficult however to remain starry-eyed about singles' clubs when you remember that the slang name for them – used by men – is 'grab a granny' clubs.

To be fair, there are people who find what they are looking for in those clubs but proportionately there are far more who are disappointed. It is best for the widowed to approach them without too high hopes. One widow said that she joined a singles' club in order to have a social life – not to find another husband.

'I enjoy going to the club and I never feel awkward there because everyone I meet is in the same boat. It is not like going to a normal party where everyone is part of a couple and you are the only odd one out. At the club no one has to explain themselves to the others. I have made friends there with people of both sexes and the club has enriched my life because it has given me a social outlet.'

Clubs like the one she joined try to avoid being smirched with the 'grab a granny' tag by refusing entry on club nights to anyone who is not a member. Exactly how this is expected to weed out all the people with less than honourable reasons for going to the club escapes me but it would certainly prevent any passer-by just dropping in on the off chance of finding some easy entertainment. A friend who joined a considerable number of singles' clubs after her divorce quickly discovered that many of the people who were there were neither separated, widowed nor divorced as the club's title implied. There was little or no surveillance of the club membership attempted. In the case of marriage bureaux, the older-established, better-recognized names do have a vetting procedure which they apply to their clients, but many, especially the 'dating' agencies, just throw people together and hope for the best. A classic case of 'caveat emptor'.

A widower told me about a man of his acquaintance who made a practice of joining singles' clubs and answering lonely hearts advertisements in search of complaisant and undemanding women. He was quite unscrupulous about the sort of woman who was his prey – 'the eager, hopeful pushovers. You can always tell them by their clothes. Homemade dresses in too-young patterns mark them out every time.'

He had worked out a method of telling whether a woman would fall into his pushover category and not cause any trouble when the affair was over.

'When he goes to her house if the lobelia is sitting up and begging in the front garden, he knows that what she wants is another husband. He calls those women domesticated hamsters, and he usually shakes her hand when she answers the door and says he has made a mistake. Then he just walks off and leaves her.'

It was difficult not to feel outrage at this unsavoury tale and I hope that if this book does nothing else it will encourage women to stand up for themselves as individuals; to develop a self-sufficiency and a pride that will prevent such things happening to them.

On two occasions I went to singles' clubs – the first time was about a year after Adam's death when I was feeling bitterly alone. A divorced neighbour, who knew every singles' club in the district, persuaded me to accompany her to a club night held in a pub near Charing Cross station. It was pouring rain that night and at the door of the hall where the club was held stood a posse of men inspecting with critical eyes every woman who went in. The atmosphere inside was one of strained and desperate jollity. Eyes darted in every direction and conversation was a mixture of suspicion and opportunism – 'Do you own your house? Have you any kids? Do you live alone?' Even my loneliness and unquenchable optimism could not stand an evening in the club and I fled from the hall, leaving my friend to her fate. In my haste to get away I left behind a new and cherished umbrella – red with a frill round it which had been given to me as a birthday present. Even the lure of my beloved brolly however could not take me back to the pub.

The second time I went to a singles' club the experience was more seemly but equally depressing. I was commissioned by a newspaper to write an article about the club which had newly opened. Everyone there was very sad though they were bearing up well, sitting around chatting bravely with glasses of beer or gin and tonics in their hands. It was obvious that they had hoped to meet someone special that night and the realization that it was unlikely to happen was dawning on them. They talked to each other about the tragedies of their lives – the wives and husbands who had run away or died, the children they had struggled to bring up alone. It seemed that the longer they sat rehashing those subjects the less likely it would be for them to break out of their chrysalides of the past. They were decent, responsible people looking for others but I felt it would have been better for them if they could all have just had a glorious knees up and got drunk together. On the way home that night I wept because going to the singles' club had made me feel lonelier and more widowed than I had felt for years.

Another way of finding 'friends' is to advertise in the lonely hearts or personal columns of magazines and newspapers. Over the last few years these columns have been appearing in a large variety of outlets which would never have considered running such advertisements before. Even the august Scottish daily the *Scotsman* has a regular crop of ads from men and women seeking the companionship of the opposite sex. It is interesting and amusing to compare the styles of advertisers in various periodicals like the *Tatler*, *Private Eye*, *Spare Rib* and the various newspapers that run a personal column. The reader must be careful that they are the correct sex for the advertiser – some shroud their preferences in circumlocution but others are more outright and the word 'gay' appears in its modern usage very frequently. It seems that there is a lonely hearts advertisement language just as there is an estate agents' language . . . 'Scope for imaginative restoration' from an estate agent's ad usually means a house that is almost derelict. 'Fun-loving' in the lonely hearts ad means someone who is looking for sex and little else.

The social backgrounds of the advertisers also are emphasized by where they place their pleas – *Tatler* ads lean heavily towards materialism and status. One lady recently advertised for a man who was interested in 'voluntary work, classical music and ski-ing' while another sought a man in 'business, a profession, a diplomat or a landowner'. *Private Eye* advertisers concentrate on the more swinging side of life and many of them are seeking what they describe as 'caring relationships'. As might be expected the great sex search has a more puritanical aspect in Edinburgh's *Scotsman*. The people advertising there are eager to present themselves as sober, responsible citizens – one advertisement that ran for several days was from a Church of Scotland minister. Another male advertiser stated the sort of car he drove in an attempt to lure suitable ladies. The essential point seems to be that if you advertise, select the sort of paper or magazine you read yourself as the advertising medium.

I was anxious to interview people who advertised to find out the response they received and answered several advertisements from men and women with a letter explaining that I was writing this book and would be interested to hear about whether their search for companionship was successful. The only reply I received came from a widow who had originally attracted my interest in the personal column of a national newspaper because she described herself as 'warm, loving and rather silent', terms which she found were open to misinterpretation by some of the people who replied to her. She turned out to be a cheerful, enthusiastic, middle-aged lady prepared openly to admit her loneliness and need for male companionship.

'After my husband died, I met a man and began having an affair with him but to my eternal shame I have to admit that he was a terrible drag and I only wanted him around for sex. The children hated Bill because they felt he was taking away some of the love that I should be giving them. The atmosphere grew so impossible that Bill said he was going to leave but I begged him to stay simply because I could not face being alone again. In the end he did leave – he ran off with one of my friends. I was furious because he had been the one to make the break and I had not had the courage to send him packing.

'I decided to advertise because I felt there would be more chance that way of finding the sort of man I really would love to meet. I tried to make my ad as specific as possible but even then a lot of replies came from people I knew would be just another Bill. The day I saw my advert in print however I felt as if I had bridged a gap with the outside world.'

She had twelve replies – a couple of which were obscene. She selected four which seemed suitable. She met the four men and in the end nothing came out of any of the meetings – except trouble with one advertiser.

'I blame myself,' she said, 'because I should not have answered his first letter. It was fourteen pages long and every now and again he had printed something like "TAKE CARE" and "REMEMBER NOT EVERYONE IS TO BE TRUSTED". It struck me that anyone so suspicious was probably not to be trusted himself. Those forebodings proved correct because after we met, I found it difficult to shake him off. In spite of precautions he found out my phone number and where I live and he rings up to say things like "You think you are clever but you won't get rid of me so easily."'

I sympathized very much with that woman, because I too had an affair with a man that I despised. From the beginning the whole thing was a disaster because he was a bore, he drank too much and embarrassed me. But I could not throw him out of my life because he filled my bed. That was all. In the end it broke up, much to my relief. I had some intimation of how near I had been to disaster when one afternoon a private detective turned up on my doorstep. He was posing as a buyer for the house next door which was up for sale at the time but there was something so suspicious and seedy about him that I suspected him of being a cruising burglar. That evening however my departed lover's wife rang up to tell me she had put a private detective on his trail. He had said that they were separated but of course that did not tie up with her interpretation of their situation. My relief at knowing our liaison was ended and there was no chance of me being landed with the incubus of the other woman's husband forever was immense and has made me extremely circumspect ever since.

It seems that the people who make the best adjustments to the problems of deprivation and loneliness are those who are pragmatists, in its 'matter of fact' definition.

In certain circles the problems of a woman on her own are solved by a man she refers to as her BF – or 'best friend'. His function in her life can range from purely being an escort, the other half of her couple and thereby her passport back into society, or it can be more intimate.

From time to time those associations are lived on very long leashes – one couple meet once a year when they go on holiday together; others arrange meetings or rendezvous only occasionally. They all say that their relationships thrive because there is no place in them for jealousy or rivalry and the problem of boredom never crops up because they are not together long enough for that. Very often the BF is a married man whose wife is either complaisant because she is unthreatened by the arrangement or who is unaware of it and the couple themselves have no desire to break up any existing arrangements.

One woman described how she found her BF.

'I was lonely for years because I was always setting my sights too high and all the men I fancied were already snapped up. I dreamt of another romance, of some splendid man coming along and sweeping me off my feet. Whenever I went out to a social occasion, I'd dress up in high hopes that this would be the day I'd find Mr Right but of course he never did materialize out of the woodwork and I'd go home again in disillusion.

'Then one night, almost by accident, I went to bed with an old friend who used to come round to cut the grass and change the plugs for me. He was an old friend of the family and I had never thought of *him* as my Mr Right. And I'm sure he had never thought of me as his ideal mistress. But amazingly it has all turned out very well. We suit each other and don't expect anything but pleasure and mutual amusement from each other. He's married and there is no way we intend to break up anyone else's life.'

She summed up the feeling of many people involved in the BF situation – 'Neither of us want continuous company, we get on far better by seeing each other regularly but with gaps in between. I have my life and he has his and in a way that makes us far more interesting to each other.'

It seems to me that this, though unconventional, is the ideal solution for loneliness and sexual deprivation in widowhood. After years of living on your own it is difficult to imagine going back to living with someone else. An old

widow was asked if she would like to have her d
miraculously returned to her and after thinking for
she said:

'I don't think so really. After all, where would he      nis
clothes?'

To think about such a mundane problem is typical of the reluctance to return to mutual dependence of people who had learned to live on their own. I am intensely gregarious, but only for part of the time; there is also a part of me now that yearns for solitude and silence and if I am deprived of it for too long because of constant company, I become tense and fractious. Happiness, I have learned, does not lie in the stereotyped ideal and having someone to share your space in the world is all very well providing you do not have to continually bump against each other. Life hardly ever works out like a 'true romance' and as you get older it seems more realistic and much funnier. After all, sex and love are part of the human comedy and to quote James Thurber: 'Humour is emotional chaos remembered in tranquillity.'

### The Maze of Confusion – Anger and Guilt

The prolonged and complicated emotional chaos that follows widowing is difficult to describe to anyone who has not experienced it for themselves. When the outside world is beginning to expect the bereaved to be recovering from the blow, what is actually happening is that they are wallowing in a sea of conflicting emotions – anger and guilt, sorrow and longing, disillusion and disbelief all crowd together in the mind. Two of the strongest feelings are anger and remorse and those are what people in sorrow find most difficult to acknowledge or rationalize.

'I felt so *angry* all the time,' said one widow. 'There was nothing specific to be angry about but I was simply raging inside.'

Anger is one of the strongest emotions experienced by the bereaved. In the initial stages it is usually directed at some outside stalking horse or object – someone or something which they feel has been instrumental in bringing about their loss. A doctor who failed to turn up in time or who seemed to make a wrong diagnosis, a hospital where the husband or wife died and which seemed cavalier in its treatment of them. Sometimes family relationships become very strained because the widow or widower conceives an anger against other family members who appear to be lacking in true grief or sympathy. Friends can be turned against for similar reasons.

It is important for the people around a widowed person to recognize that anger is more healthy if it can be openly expressed. If it is denied at source or subdued it can emerge later as a more destructive, corrosive power. 'Anger repressed only leads to severe depression,' said a psychiatric social worker. It also leads to deep set misery and bitterness and everyone knows the 'brave little widow' who spends the rest of her life 'bearing up against adversity'.

'What you cannot cure you must endure. When I reach the end of my tether I just tie a knot in the rope and hang on,' said an example of this.

Bitterness too – which is resignation carried to extremes – only leads to an increase in isolation. And it is hard not to be envious of less unfortunate people around you.

Early in widowhood I was plagued by the feeling that there were many couples of my acquaintance who would find the death of one of them almost a release – 'Remember statistics show that one in four marriages in England and one in three in Scotland end in divorce. So it is only to be expected that every widowing is not a cause for grief,' said a doctor. Why then, I wondered, did death have to take away my husband who I had loved so much? It was only when I was able to face up to the anger that made me feel that, did the danger of it turning into a general bitterness disappear.

It seems to be essential to find a personal target for anger, at least in the first stage of widowing. My stalking horse was my husband's company who I felt had been insensitive in their treatment of us and thereby, I thought, dismissive of Adam himself. A few weeks after his death I was asked to go to the company offices to sign a paper saying that at no time in the future would I ask them for any help – after the insurance money was settled in a trust for us. When I was there I was also asked to take home with me some of the things in Adam's old office. The managing director rang a bell for his secretary and said, 'Mrs So-and-so would you fetch Mr Taylor's things out of Mr Reid's office.'

I realized that the water had well and truly closed over Adam – even his office was now known as someone else's. It would have been a good deal more tactful if it had been referred to as 'Mr Taylor's old office'; that would not have hurt so much. How difficult he would have found it to believe that the business ran on so smoothly without him. I was given a plastic bag containing some cufflinks and pens along with a selection of foreign coins, a few dog-eared papers and visiting cards. 'We have kept anything relating to company business,' I was told, and the selection had been already made without me having any part in it. When I left the managing director's office I was seething with rage though I did not immediately understand why. As I stood at the lift gate, the secretary who had accompanied me out, put her hand on my arm and said, 'I understand what you are feeling, I'm a widow myself you see.' It was the only sign of compassion I received in that office.

For years afterwards I *hated* the company with a terrible loathing which can only have done me good because it provided an outlet for all my other feelings of anger. I read the stock market pages of the newspaper every day hoping their shares would fall and if they did, my spirits rose childishly in delight. In time I forgot all about it, however, my rage had dissipated. At least it dissipated as far as the company was concerned. What was more upsetting however was the feeling that I was carrying a repressed scream inside me. It was difficult for me to work out exactly what I was angry *about* – until I realized it was against Adam himself.

The first articulation of this was the day when I heard my mind asking myself – 'Why did he have to die and leave me to cope on my own?' In a way, when trouble struck, it seemed as if he had chosen the easy way out by dying. I was also resentful that he had failed to leave a will or to make any provision for what would happen to us if he died. Inevitably I thought, 'If making a will had been one of his business responsibilities it would certainly have been done most efficiently.' In fact Adam was not unique in dying intestate and it is astonishing how few people take the trouble to make a will until they are fairly well advanced in age. A recent survey pointed out that only some 24 per cent of husbands and 10 per cent of wives had made a will. The proportion is lowest among people under thirty – only 7 per cent of them make wills – until when they reached seventy, the proportion rises to over 40 per cent. People often console themselves that they need not bother making wills because they have little to leave or because the laws of intestacy will cope with their estates quite efficiently. In fact any family left without a will being made by the husband is almost inevitably going to be forced into expensive legal involvement whereas if a will is in existence, the legal costs of administering it will be much smaller. The main reason why people do not make wills however is that they think they are immortal and are reluctant to consider the possibility of their own death. Adam fell into the category of people who simply closed their eyes to facts and decided to think about such unpleasant matters as making a will at some time in the distant future.

In spite of myself my resentment against Adam for not making a will led me on to recollect other past derelictions and shortcomings on his part. I remembered things he had said or done which had rankled at the time and my resentment was always worse if I had swept them aside in my mind when they happened. Suddenly it seemed as if I had forgotten nothing – only put it into a corner to be resurrected later. I remembered his reluctance to share in family outings, how he hated picnics and refused to go on them, how the children were only allowed to travel in his car under constant surveillance and if they dropped a sweet paper or made a noise, he would accuse me of not being able to keep them in order. I couldn't and I knew I couldn't and the anxiety of trying to appease him as well as keep them quiet made me dread our all going out together. I remembered the time he said, during an argument about household bills, 'If I didn't have you and the children to keep, I'd be a very rich bachelor.' That remark seared me because I *did* feel guilty of riding through life on another person's coat-tails,

I *did* resent spending money that was not my own and I *did* feel like a non-productive parasite. It is always remarks that strike nearest home that are the most hurtful. I have heard that couples coming up to a divorce are able to remember every minute insult and hurt from their married life – things that were taken in their stride when they were united in love. Now I was in the process of divorcing myself from the memory of a dead man. Though it was brutal, it was therapeutic. My resurrection of past hurts and angers was almost pleasant – I indulged myself in them in the same way as someone who is addicted to eating chocolate goes on gorging until they feel sick. It was like a vice; from the deepest recesses of my memory, I brought out and dangled more and more skeleton memories.

And all this time I still missed him bitterly. The paradox of my situation was totally unexpected. I frequently had the most vivid dreams about him – for the first few months of widowhood my subconscious mind refused to accept the knowledge of his death and I dreamed as if he was still alive. I would awake tranquil and content with the memory of them – until a slow dawning of the truth came with my returning consciousness. I would slide my hand over to his side of the bed and find it empty.

When I progressed to the stage of remembering old resent-ments, however, my dreams changed. Then I had vivid dreams of him returning with reassuring explanations of his absence. They were very vivid dreams – he would always appear in the doorway wearing his grey business suit and carrying his brief-case. Tanned and grinning, he would be full of chatter, ex-plaining that he had been on a prolonged business trip; his plane had crashed in the desert; once he even said he had been in jail. I accepted all those explanations as perfectly reasonable and was overjoyed at his return. He was back and that was all that mattered but of course I still had to cope with the awful awakenings in the morning.

It took five years before I dug down to the final strata of my repressed anger and the length of time must be excused by the fact that I was then coming on memories which I did not want to acknowledge to myself. I knew they were there and I was reluctant to disinter them, but I was not going to recover from widowing until I did.

Although I do not belong to any religion, I was brought up in the grey bleakness of Scottish Calvinism and one of my early memories is of being taken to church and hearing a preacher expound on the fires of Hell that awaited every sinner. I could vividly imagine the fires, leaping high to the church roof and consuming everyone inside it. I did not know exactly what sin was but I was fully aware of the danger of inadvertently committing one.

When I married, it mattered a lot to me that we had taken solemn vows and although I have never been conventionally jealous I was totally possessive of my husband and refused to consider the idea that he might ever be unfaithful to me. That would have been a mortal blow to my pride as well as to my love for him. Now I know that of course I was deceiving myself and I think I knew at the time although I refused to look facts in the face. Before he died, Adam had tried to talk to me about it but I turned him aside because I did not feel ready to cope with any confessions he wanted to make. I was unable to predict how I would react.

When I began thinking about this as a widow, however, I was able to remember people, places and incidents which should have fitted together in a jigsaw of suspicion at the time.

I remembered the strained periods when our marriage was definitely going through troubled times. I could even pin-point when it now seemed almost certain he was involved in some affair. The anger I felt about all this almost burned out the most hysterical aspects of my mourning. I longed to know every detail of what had actually happened. It was utter frustration to think that I had been acting in a human drama of which I was totally unaware – or which I refused to acknow-ledge. I longed above all to talk to him about it, to charge him with my suspicions and upbraid him with my reproaches. My egotism was badly bruised and my picture of what my marriage had been like was radically altered. I was now looking at it as if I was an outsider.

Only then was I able to recognize that he must have felt the constraints of domesticity very badly and he probably felt justification for what he did. I knew too that he felt remorse because of the way he tried to broach the subject with me in the year before he died. I now saw my husband as he had truly been, not as I had manufactured him in my mind, and strangely I was able to love him more but in a less possessive way. I was also saddened by the thought that he had probably loved someone else as well as me and I won-dered if she had loved him too. If she had, how did she learn of his death, how did she feel about it? Perhaps she did not even know that he had died. I wondered who she was. In a strange way I would like to meet her and talk to her about him, not in jealousy or in rivalry but in the knowledge that we both had loved him. There must be a link between us, whoever or wherever she is.

When I eventually reached this stage of tranquillity after months of anguished remembering, I had my last dream about

Adam. He came back again and when I saw him standing at the door, I went up to him, kissed his cheek and put my hand on his arm:

'Darling you can't come back,' I told him. 'Everyone knows that I'm a widow now so you will have to go away.'

For the first time my awakening from a dream of him was peaceful and untortured. I had accepted what had happened and so had he.

A conversation I recently had with a widowed friend showed me that this form of emotional dissection is not unusual. She too felt emerging anger against her late husband though there was no question that she had not loved him and did so still. What she was talking about was the second stage of anger when she had begun rehashing old resentments.

'I often remember how he once said to me that I had never known what it was like to have to struggle or to have problems,' she said. 'That really rankled because he chose to ignore the very real problems I have had – we were eternally hard up, I struggled to keep the family going when he lost his job and when he had his first illness, we had two babies who died at birth – and yet he could turn round and say that I had never had any problems! Not only did we have all the things I've listed but I also had to put up with his unfaithfulness, but he ignored that too.

'Now I sometimes wish he could come back so that I could say "So I've never had any problems have I?" I'd like him to see how I've brought up the children, got myself a job and made myself financially independent. I'd just like the chance to present him with all those things that I've done since he died.'

I recognized what she was saying because I've said it all myself. In the end she will adjust her memories and dismiss her resentments but there is still the last stage to go through because by starting to question things that were said between them, she is only lifting the edge of her anger. That is the worst hurdle of all to get over because it entails anger against yourself and it also means that you have to look at your marriage through another person's eyes.

It took me a long time to work through to the end of my angers, and perhaps a series of sessions on a psychiatrist's couch would have got me there sooner, but at least by doing it myself I was able to cover the ground at my own pace and, once covered, there was no need to retrace my steps. Too deep introspection can be dangerous but in the case of adjusting to a terrible blow, I think it cannot do harm unless it is allowed to become hysterical. Hidden feelings must be examined honestly, even if what you are acknowledging is not to your own credit, to enable you to come to some acceptance of the situation.

I was once told, 'All mourning is a fake really, what you are really crying about is yourself.' But anyone who was concerned only for themselves would not inflict such suffering on themselves and they would certainly not allow themselves to expose their deepest feelings in such agony. After mourning is over, in its place is a deep sense of loss that can stay with you forever but need not necessarily make you unhappy. In a strange way it can be life enhancing for, like someone who has had a great religious experience, you are party to one of life's great secrets. You have known and come to terms with loss.

You will only come to this realization however if you are capable of examining yourself and asking, 'What is happening? Why do I feel the way I do?' Open your mind, be as honest to yourself as you can and you will find the answer.

Guilt is another emotion that confuses the reactions of people to grief. It is an almost inescapable part of sorrow. When a mother or father dies, their children very often mourn them with regret for not being more understanding or demonstrative towards them while alive, and this sad remorse is openly recognized by the mourners because they know it is common and to be expected.

The guilt that comes with widowing is, however, much more complicated. Like anger, once it is acknowledged and grappled with, the sooner it disappears and the mourner is reconciled to the reasons why it appeared in the first place.

After my article on widowhood was published a letter arrived, ten pages long and closely written, which came from a widow who was so agonized by guilt that she was on the verge of total breakdown. She wrote about all her own shortcomings towards her husband in detail – how she failed to recognize his growing frailty and forced him to go on a holiday that brought about his fatal stroke, and from there she travelled back to every oversight she had committed on him during their married life of almost fifty years. She had persuaded herself that their whole time together had been a charade with her dominating and exploiting her husband.

'I think we must have been incompatible and it was me who was wrong,' she wrote. She also said that her behaviour was alienating her family and friends and it was not difficult to understand how this would happen when reading the repetitive and inconsolable letter. Her conflicts were brought about by the dawning realization that she too had faults. Neither would she accept that when people are loved even their shortcomings are taken into account. It was also probable that her obsessive guilt had deeper roots than she was able to acknowledge in the letter and until she faced up to what they were her pointless round of self-recrimination about small things would never end.

Generally, guilt is pinned on to a specific incident. Widows and widowers can blame themselves for not seeking medical help quickly enough; for not insisting on a 'second opinion' which many bereaved people seem to think would have prevented a death. The apparent arbitrariness of heart attacks in young men worried me very much after Adam died – had I failed to read the signs in him? Could I have in some way prevented what happened? I also felt a terrible guilt about the fact that he had to die alone. If only I had been with him. I at least could have helped him to die. It was the last thing I would have been able to do for him, I said to myself many times. I mentioned this feeling to my doctor and he said, 'If it was going to happen there was very little you could have done about it at any time. He could have died sitting on the sofa in your sitting-room without you being aware of what had happened.' It also helped me when I realized that no matter where you are or who you are with, dying is something you must do alone.

My second feeling of guilt was more difficult to rationalize. It was always Adam who had to say 'I love you' first – my Calvinist repressions prevented me from being the most outgoing. Even on our last conversation together when he telephoned me from Singapore on the night before he died, it had to be him who said 'I love you' and me who only answered 'I love you too'. Why could I, for once, not have been the one to say it first?

This feeling of failure gradually extended to a feeling of more seriously having let him down – had I in some way abandoned him to death? Had I given him up to it, allowed it to happen almost by some sort of witchcraft? Like the last stage of anger, this last stage of guilt was very upsetting to me until I realized that the state of widowhood carries with it an overwhelming sense of somehow being to blame for what has happened – the widow is affected by a primitive, age old taboo.

For many centuries and in many cultures, the widow has been a figure of dread, a reminder of death. Society shuns her as if she carries round with her some contagion of sorrow and death.

There are now many things that we look on as backward or ridiculous – bastardy is no longer the permanent blight on the life of an unfortunate child. When Lord Byron's illegitimate daughter Allegra died she could not be buried in a consecrated churchyard. In the past bastards had a load of guilt handed down to them as a birthright, and today widows still carry guilt around with them as a legacy.

I once heard a man talking about a woman who had married twice and both husbands had died.

'I'd steer clear of her,' he said, only half joking. It was as if he felt she put a death curse on any man who associated with her. Yet my own great-grandfather married three times and was contemplating a fourth bride when he died himself – no one ever suggested that he was bad luck for women and if I tell anyone about him today, they laugh and say 'Lucky old devil'.

The widow, however, is a sinister figure, set apart both as a figure of pity and of fear. Even in some Hindu sects today widows are regarded as inauspicious except to their own children and must be kept apart from the outside world. An Indian widow cannot attend any family celebrations because her very presence casts a blight on the proceedings. She may marry very young and her husband may have died before she even reached puberty – yet she is still a widow and banned from marrying again. She can be doomed to a life in a plain white sari, working as a domestic help in the family of her in-laws, shunned and denigrated by everyone.

It is hardly surprising that in the past some widows preferred to commit suttee on the funeral pyres of their husbands – a quick death would seem preferable to a long drawn out misery. Suttee is now officially banned in India but even today there are cases of it reported in the newspapers as having happened in remote parts of the country. Often suttee was forced on a woman by the family who did not want to feed an unproductive and sinister mouth for years to come.

The practice of suttee can be traced back for thousands of years to very early civilizations – it is thought to have taken place in Ur of the Chaldees; the ancient Chinese practised it, so did nomads of Central Asia and some early Indo-European civilizations. The word 'suttee' itself though now applied to the act of widow burning actually means 'a virtuous woman' which gives some idea of the social pressures there were on widows to remove themselves from the world when their husbands died. In theory in Indian society the committing of suttee was always voluntary but long ago in practice, especially in the high castes, it was virtually obligatory. Records of Viking burials too make special note that one of the wives of the man who died was burned with him – they were given the choice of who was to have the honour. An Arab commentator who wrote down his observations of a Viking funeral, however, said how the woman to be burned changed her mind at the critical point but was thrown on to the fire nonetheless. Widows in European society are not doomed to simultaneous death with their husbands but they are certainly consigned to a state of social suttee – they are still figures of unacknowledged dread both to themselves and to other people.

At a friend's home some years ago I met a young and beautiful woman who was very bright and sparkling. She told me about her husband who was an airline pilot and who travelled abroad a great deal but, she said, he was returning home soon and it was always marvellous when they were together. I was recently widowed then and it was difficult not to feel a twinge of envy at her happiness. But when I was leaving my hostess detained me in the hall and asked if the stranger had talked to me about her husband. When I said she had, she shook her head.

'I don't suppose she told you he was killed in a car crash last month.'

The young woman had steadfastly refused to acknowledge the terrible thing that had happened, she could not face the cold realization that she was a widow and was building a wall of self-deception around herself. The state of widowhood was too terrible for her to contemplate. My friend lost contact with that young woman and I do not know what happened to her. Whatever it was must have been traumatic.

Literature is full of examples of the traditional, fearful view of widows. The poet Robert Lowell wrote a telling line – 'The Black Widow, death.' He puts together three awful images – the colour black, the final end, death, and the sinister figure of the widow.

The word 'widow' comes from 'vidoy' a corruption of the French word 'vide' – empty. The French 'vide' in its turn is linked to a Sanskrit word for separation and desolation. In early times the word 'widow' was applied to both sexes and a widower was the agency of death – a sword, for example, could be a widower. Later however only women were given the name 'widow' and men became 'widowers' and there are no references in literature to their untouchability, to the necessity for celibacy being forced on them and they are not the butt of jokes the way that widows have been.

For things that are dreaded are often joked about and guilt and resentment are only increased when a woman realizes that overnight she has not only become an object of pity but a potential figure of fun. Dickens portrayed a 'funny' widow in Mrs Bardell who tries to ensnare Mr Pickwick into marriage and when she fails, sues him for breach of promise. The dread of widows is illustrated, also in *Pickwick Papers,* when Sam Weller's father advises his son – 'Be werry careful o' vidders all your life.'

The 'be careful o' vidders' advice is taken by men and women today who still see the widow as a predator, set to worm or trick her way back into the pair-oriented society. The widow herself is not expected to feel any resentment about her new status; in a way, society feels, she has brought it on herself by marrying a man who died. Much of the guilt experienced by widows stems from their own divided feelings about this, by their conditioning and by their inherited prejudices.

The 'respectable' widow is also a well-known fictional character – always mourning, discreet, celibate and resigned. A poem entitled 'The Farm Widow' by Maurice Lindsay describes a typical example.

Her skirts bustled
with decent pride; alone since the day the tractor
hauled itself up the field on the hill and toppled.

The widow in the poem makes a frugal living by selling eggs to passers-by and the customers watched her counting out their change with

. . . silent pity
then sensed she wasn't wanting
in anything they could offer; that she seemed
like one whom life had used too soon for writing
some sort of purpose with.

That is the awful condemnation – 'life had used too soon . . .' Widows should never have to accept that death sentence any more than they have to accept suttee. If they are seventeen or seventy, they have a right to their lives. There is no reason why a widow cannot be as happy, outrageous and self-determining as any other woman. If it is in her make-up or if she chooses she can be flirtatious or flibbertigibbet, aggressive or inconsequential. Her life, her hopes, her ambitions need not come to an end because the person she loved was so unfortunate as to die.

A more acceptable fictional widow prototype than the Farm Widow is Chaucer's Wife of Bath, a randy, Rabelaisian lady with an uncomplicated attitude to the world. She married several times and felt no shame about doing so – it was unreasonable in her book for a woman to have to resign herself to a life of mourning and celibacy. She told the party of pilgrims going to Canterbury that if her present husband was to die, she would just look for another to take his place, church consecrated or not. This was flying directly in the face of conventional Christian teaching which advocated celibacy as a more admirable way of life than marriage. Libertinism is not my prescription for happy widowhood but the Wife of Bath is worthy of admiration because of her refusal to knuckle down, to do what was expected of her.

Another widowed voice from the past is that of Christine de Pisan, who lived and worked as a poet and song writer in the French court.

Christine's authentic and moving observations on widowhood come down to us today through translations of her works which Barbara Tuchman quoted in her book *A Distant Mirror* – an account of the fourteenth century in Europe. Miss Tuchman notes that Christine de Pisan is significant as a protester for the rights of women – and of widows. She was a career woman who worked to support herself and her three children after her husband died. She wrote songs and poems which were popular among the courtiers who thronged round King Charles V of France and in many of them Christine's authentic voice still comes through –

> No one knows the labour my poor heart endures
> To dissimulate my grief when I find no pity.
> The less sympathy in friendship, the more cause for tears.
> So I make no plaint of my piteous mourning
> But laugh when I would rather weep,
> And without rhyme or rhythm make my songs
> To conceal my heart.

Every widow who fights her way out of sorrow knows what Christine de Pisan means when she talks about laughing to conceal her heart. She also suffered from the feeling that women, and widows, were inferior beings and in one of her songs wonders why men are 'so unanimous in attributing wickedness to women . . . since we were also created by God'.

Today we have learned that there is no guilt in being born female. The next step is for widows to realize there is no guilt in having lost the person they loved.

# 7

Religion and Other Consolations

THE Italian proverb 'In prosperity, no altars smoke' sums up a very normal tendency not to bother about propitiating the gods or seeking religion until the need is urgent. In my own case, altars did not smoke in times of prosperity nor have they smoked a great deal since.

The theoretical study of religion has always fascinated me but as far as finding a personal belief is concerned, the question of continuance after death has always been the hurdle that brings me down. My agnosticism began at school when I realized it was impossible to go on believing in the same un-questioning, round-eyed way as I had done while a child at Sunday School. I announced my conversion to Buddhism when Buddhists were as remote from everyday, small town Scottish life as visitors from outer space but my decision to adopt it as my faith owed more to a desire to escape the boredom of religious instruction – which was purely based on Christian-ity then – than to true revelation. In time my Buddhist phase also wore off. At university I studied history and was particularly attracted by the medieval period when religion was of para-mount importance. Abstruse wrangles between scholar clerics fascinated me – I could understand their anxieties to find out how many angels can dance on the head of a pin. It was easier to appreciate the individual positions of men like Bernard of Clairvaux and Peter Abelard if you took into consideration the human drives that were in the men themselves and also if you were able to maintain an attitude of dispassionate observation. The arguments that filled the halls of twelfth-century Paris appealed to me as purely intellectual exercises and not as vast divisions of faith.

Adam, however, had been a convinced Christian and when he died I desperately wanted to believe in his God – even if only for his sake. Surely this would be the time when there would be some sign of the continuance of man's soul? I longed for some reassurance that he had not just been snuffed out like a candle for that would be a cruel betrayal of every belief he had held – but no sign came. Try as I could, my own position has remained the same as that of Cyril Connolly who summed up his belief as 'love, poetry and doubt' – for me, above all, doubt.

A friend who was concerned at my lack of faith gave me a selection of books to read through which I carefully searched for some sign that would shake my disbelief. The only books that impressed me were those of the late Professor William Barclay, a man of compassion and burning conviction, but though I felt admiration for the man and his writing, his truth was still not my truth. There is absolutely no point in trying to pretend, even to yourself, that you have a faith when you do not. True belief is a consolation deep inside you and I have the utmost respect and even envy for those who have it. Unfortunately I do not share it myself.

After Adam's funeral I went to church several times because I felt great gratitude to Dr McCluskey, the minister who had conducted the service. If anyone could have convinced me that God does exist it was him but though I admired his sermons, my last vestigial hope for belief finally flickered and died. When I eventually consciously accepted the idea that I was without hope for religious consolation, I was in a strange way freed from some of my anguish. The railing against God dropped away. How can you complain against a God in which you do not believe? Now that I am sure there is nothing but the darkness of eternity in front of me and that my only hope of immortality lies in my children, I have a serenity and acceptance about dying. While I still doubted, fear of death used to terrify me. When I was dropping off to sleep at night, the spectre of it used sometimes to rise up in my mind . . . the terror of a world without *me* in it, my own total annihilation, and I would sit up in bed shouting to myself, 'Stop it, stop it.' Once I fully accepted the idea of oblivion however there were no terrors left and the accepted idea meant that I was determined to live my life to its fullest extent.

Researching this book, I consulted a priest about the problem of consolation for people with religious doubts and he said that it was presumptuous of anyone who had little faith before a death to expect to find miraculous spiritual comfort afterwards.

'Faith does not just appear as if by magic at times of trouble,' he explained. 'You can only build on the ground of what has gone before.'

Perhaps in this age of disillusion, that explains why many people told me about their lack of spiritual comfort when the person they loved died. They all admitted that religion had been little more than a lip service irrelevancy in their lives before trouble hit them.

A widower explained: 'The vicar did not seem to want to know me after my wife died. I had not been a regular church goer but she had gone from time to time and taken the children with her. In spite of that he never came to see us after the funeral but I don't expect I had any right to think he would really. There was no comfort for me in the thought she had gone to heaven or anything like that. I have not gone to church since, her death put all idea of church going out of my head.'

Several widows also agreed that the orthodox beliefs they had unquestioningly held – or thought they had held – since childhood, also helped them little.

'Quite frankly the church was a dead loss for me,' said one woman. 'I was a comparative stranger in the place we were living when my husband died and the local priest did his duty but little more. It was the ordinary people of the village who consoled me – they were more Christian in their attitudes than the man who represented the church.'

Significantly all statements of disillusion came from members of the Presbyterian or Anglican religions. Those who stated with certainty that their belief had helped them through bereavement were all Roman Catholics. The playwright Jean Kerr summed up their attitude:

'The most important thing about me is that I'm a Catholic. It is a superstructure within which you can work, like a sonnet.'

A widow talked about this 'sonnet superstructure'.

'I have been a keen church goer all my life and my religion did not fail me when I needed it most. I know with certainty that I will see my husband again but I have only one problem – I often worry about how I am going to recognize him. You see the body is cast off like a suit of old clothes and only the spirit goes on. When I first looked at his dead body I thought

"How am I going to live the rest of my life without you?" but then I realized I was being stupid for I know that when my own life is finished we will meet again. Hanging on to the idea that death is only a beginning makes living without someone you love very much easier.'

Prayer was a great solace to that widow and she keeps a prayer scrapbook. When she hears about another widow or widower in sorrow, she copies out one of the prayers that helped her and sends it to them.

'I pray a lot. I talk to God about all sorts of things. It is almost as if we had a hot line to each other. Praying for me is like cleaning my teeth for it is so much part of my life. It is a wonderful solace and I really feel joyous after prayer.'

A Roman Catholic widower had a more subtle but equally satisfying result from his religion.

'My children and I benefited greatly from our Catholic background. The nuns in the hospital where my wife died were a great help and it was one of them who pointed out to me that death is a matter of Christian will – trying to rationalize it is like trying to rationalize something that is completely illogical. I had expected that if my wife died, my faith would be shaken because I prayed constantly while she was ill that she would be spared. However, when she did die, I did not feel as if God had failed me. In a way I felt as if my prayers had been answered and my faith was unchanged. I am comforted by the certainty that we will meet again. A few years ago I went to Austria and saw the Von Trapp motto carved up over the door of their house – "God Has No Reason". It seemed so true that I have adopted it as my own.'

Such serene acceptance is rare but everyone needs consolation of some sort and the search for it often takes people to other reassurances. For a time doctors had the traditional listening role of the priest thrust on them but it seems that in recent years, they too have been found inadequate. The methods of conventional medicine are being continually questioned and the indiscriminate handing out of tranquillizers has been found to solve no problems. Sleeping pills and tranquillizers muffle the emotions but the pain and suffering is still there inside. People often seek psychiatric help and one psychotherapist who has been in practice for more than twenty years and who sees many people suffering from grief, said that lack of religious consolation was in some way contributing to his workload.

'A few years ago people used to come to me raging against God who they felt had let them down,' he said. 'But God does not figure large in the problems of my patients any more. I think the worst agonies of grief could be ameliorated if people could find spiritual help and it is a pity that the full burial service is so little used today. If the bereaved could sit quietly and listen to what it says they might be able to derive some consolation from the words – a large part of their doubt and suffering could be soothed and they would be more accepting.'

The minister in charge of a large rural parish agreed with this and said that he always tried to include words of comfort in burial services which he conducts.

'I always include part of St Paul's Letter to the Romans,' he said, 'the bit beginning "Then what can separate us from the love of Christ? For I am convinced there is nothing in death or life, in the realm of the spirits or supernatural powers, in the world as it is or the world as it shall be, in the forces of the universe, in the heights or the depths, nothing in all creation that can separate us from the love of God."'

He also includes verses from St John, the ones that tell the mourners – 'Let not your heart be troubled'.

'For,' he added, 'if there is any sense in religion in life, it is quite illogical to think the soul will disappear into nothing.'

That minister also follows up his thoughtful funeral service with a regular programme of visiting the bereaved family, whether they were regular attenders of his church or not. He continues his visits for several months, until he feels they are no longer needed and he is always ready to give help or advice and above all to talk about the person who has died.

'Families are always eager to talk and I make a point of bringing up the name of the dead person, because it is stupid to imagine that you can just remove a personality overnight and never refer to them again.'

Before he took over his country church, that minister had worked in an industrial city and he noticed differences between reactions to death in the two communities.

'Country people have a greater acceptance of death even if they are not more obviously religious than city people. It is because they have a closer link with nature and that gives them a basic spirituality. People in the country have a strong idea of a deity even when they do not go to church. The word God has no meaning if you have no concept of what is conveyed by it. There has to be some degree of mutual experience between a priest and his people even if it is on a mystical level.

'In the city, people are cut off from this basic knowledge and their reactions to death are more traumatic at first than the reactions of country people. I have a mental picture of the town widow as opposed to the country widow. The town widow is a pitiful crumpled figure at the side of the fire with a cup of tea and a cigarette. The country widow is prouder and more stoical, more determined to put on a brave face. Unfortunately often the country widow's reactions are more delayed and worse in the end than the town widow's. It is part of my job now to help the country widow to weep.'

This sense of achieving a purpose through religion is shared by the man who works as a lay preacher among the fishing people of north-east Scotland. The fishing community have a long tradition of coping with sudden death and traumatic bereavement and they are intensely withdrawn and secretive people, reluctant to allow a newcomer into their society but in spite of that, the pastor has become a man they rely on at times of trouble. Many times he has been instrumental in bridging the gap between desolation and a return to normal life for a woman whose husband has been drowned.

He talked about a recent, typical case:

'One young woman was in a very bad way when her man was drowned. It was a great struggle to convince her that there was still a life ahead of her and that people would want to know her for herself. Without help I think she would have dropped out of life completely. My happiest day recently was when she ran up to me in the street to show me her new engagement ring. She has met another man and they will marry soon. I was very honoured to be allowed to share her happiness and to know that any help I gave her has been so well repaid.'

Everyone however is not able to receive consolation of the spiritual kind from their church and many turn to other sources of comfort. Self-awareness is now a cult on its own and people in grief often find release in various kinds of therapy — they find people to whom they can talk about their problems and in some cases they can even act out their anguish. The benefit for them is in being able to understand and articulate why they feel as they do and once this hurdle is passed, they can often go on to rebuild their lives on a new base. It is not only the young who find comfort in the new cults. Not long ago I visited a Tibetan Buddhist centre at Eskdalemuir in the South of Scotland where I was surprised to find a large part of the community were people in their middle age or even older. Some of them had given up their previous lives entirely but others were only there in retreat for a fixed period of time, regathering their resources. The atmosphere of the centre was markedly serene and tranquil, the perfect place to heal psychic wounds.

It is not uncommon for the widowed also to search for solace in the occult sciences or in the paranormal. A widow who was having a great deal of trouble recovering from the death of her husband said that one evening a visiting friend suddenly asked her, 'Did your husband smoke a pipe?'

The widow said, 'I was surprised at this because my friend had scarcely known my husband but I agreed that he did indeed smoke a pipe. She then asked me if he wore certain types of clothes and described them to me – corduroy trousers and a checked shirt. I said they were the sort of things he was in the habit of wearing in the garden or when we were sitting together at home in the evening. At that she put her hand on my arm and said "I don't want you to be frightened but he is standing behind you now with his arm along the back of your chair as if he is protecting you. He looks very happy." That experience has given me the most marvellous feeling of peace and happiness and now when I am working around the house, I can feel him with me.'

Another widow described her deep misery after her husband's death and said, 'I could not be reassured that we would meet again and the thought of losing him forever was more than I could bear. I asked my minister about it but what he said was far from convincing – it sounded like a lot of wishful thinking. The whole thing became an obsession with me. Then, by chance, I picked up a book in the library that had been written by a minister of religion whose wife had died and who received a series of strange and very comforting messages from her. The book was called *Venture Into Immortality* and it was the answer to all my questions. I got in touch with the author and he put me in touch with a medium who had helped him contact his dead wife. Eventually I consulted the medium myself and what he told me was tremendously convincing – little things that could only have come from my husband, private jokes we shared and the places we went to on our honeymoon, things that even my children did not know. I have been utterly comforted and now know that if I have to go on living for another twenty years we will catch up with each other again.'

Both of those women had been in states bordering on clinical depression when they reached the comfort of paranormal experiences. How valid these are is questionable but the benefit that the women derived from them is undeniable.

Even more sceptical people can be left in a state of hopeful doubt by psychic experiences. A widow was told by a neighbour that while the neighbour was at a seance, the widow's phone number was called out and the medium said that her husband wanted to contact her and ask for her forgiveness.

'What my neighbour did not know was that before he died my husband had gone away with another woman,' said the widow. 'Half of me thought her story sheer nonsense but there is still a little bit of me that wonders if there might not be something in it.'

A widow in her seventies wrote to a spiritualist organization after her husband's death asking for some reassurance about what had happened to him. In reply she received a letter assuring her that he was happy and was able to communicate with her via a medium. She was told not to worry and that they would meet again 'though not for a long time'.

'But there was one thing about the letter that bothered me,' she said. 'In it my husband continually referred to me as "Edie", a name I have never been called by him or anyone else. My Christian name is Edith but I've always been called by a family nickname. I signed my original letter with Edith, however.'

The growing awareness that people who are bereaved need consolation and counselling has brought about the emergence of bereavement counselling services both in Britain and abroad. In Britain, hospices for the dying warn the families of patients about their unexpected reactions to death. One of the doctors working in such a hospice said:

'We give the families permission to mourn and we have seen that where mourning begins in advance of death, the shock when it comes is not nearly so damaging, long-lasting or severe. Anticipatory mourning helps families adjust to what lies ahead. We are also able to forewarn them of some of the more bizarre and unexpected aspects of grief and when people know in advance what to expect, the problems are more easily surmounted.'

In Israel, bereavement services were originally set up to assist the families of the men killed in the fighting there and the work they did has begun to bring to light the complex patterns that grief follows. Other bereavement counselling services have been established in Sydney, Australia; in Denver, New York and Boston in the USA and in London.

Originally bereavement services in the USA were attached to hospitals where families of terminally ill patients were forewarned about the reactions they might expect to the death. The mourners were then followed up if they fell into a category of 'high risk', those whose families were unsupportive, whose lives were complicated by traumas other than the death and where bereavements were sudden or especially traumatic. Clients of these counselling services were not only the widowed but also parents mourning dead children or people mourning the death of their parents.

Since the first work in bereavement counselling began, its benefits for a wider section of the population than 'high risk' people has been recognized. Colin Murray Parkes set up his pioneering counselling service in the London borough of Camden many years ago and it has since been copied at the boroughs of Hammersmith and Barnet. Most of the staff in the centres are trained volunteers and the clients are referred to them by doctors, social workers, religious bodies and hospitals. They are able to see and to help people who would not be sufficiently disturbed by grief to need psychiatric treatment but who can assuage and come to terms with their grief by the help of sympathetic listening. One of the original helpers at the Camden centre was Mrs Lilah Kosky who realized that there was a need for such a service in her own Jewish community. She pioneered the London Jewish Bereavement Counselling Service and there are plans to start a similar one in Birmingham.

Mrs Kosky described the help that counsellors can extend to the bereaved.

'We just talk to them or let them talk to us. People in grief need to be reassured that their reactions are normal and understandable. They can talk to us about their feelings of rage and anger and we are trained to keep a calm face that is greatly reassuring. Sometimes the families of the people who come are unable to reassure them because they cannot appreciate what is happening in the minds of sufferers from severe grief. And families can sometimes be very frightened by the intensity of feeling and sometimes angered because rage is often directed against the family itself. It is difficult for people who are too close to be tolerant.

'People who come to us are often afraid that they are on the verge of a nervous breakdown and their families share that fear. When a widow or a widower starts to talk they often break down and tell us how they fear for their own sanity because they are having hallucinations about seeing the person who has died or feeling the touch of their hand and hearing their voice. Because of our training we know that this is a fairly common thing with the newly widowed and we can tell them so. Very many people are shocked and frightened by those strange experiences and unable to share their fears with family or friends but when they talk to us, we can reassure them.'

The balm of a listening and uncritical ear can help to heal the wound of mourning and it is to be hoped that the idea of bereavement counselling services will in time be more widespread.

# 8

❧❧❧

# *The New Identity*

As the months and years of my widowhood passed, without realizing it, I was rebuilding my life. From time to time there were hiccups – bad ones some of them – when I was plunged deeply back into grief and the same despair as I had felt in the beginning, but on the whole progress was continuous.

The first essential for me was to feel that I had some useful function in the world. There were times as a married woman when I had felt deeply unfulfilled and when my spirits were low it felt as if all my early education, my once high hopes and ambition had been for nothing. After widowhood however the whole perspective changed, perhaps because I no longer had the time for wasteful self-pity. I had to make a living but I wanted to do it in some way that would also give me personal fulfilment. I initially wanted to study medicine because the apparently symptomless deterioration of my husband's heart to a point when it simply stopped beating preyed deeply on my mind and it seemed a useful crusade to find out why it had happened and perhaps to prevent it happening to other people. But my age and my lack of finances prevented me from doing this and I knew that any career I chose would have to be something I could do and look after my children at the same time.

Before marriage I had worked as a newspaper reporter, for journalism had always seemed glamorous and exciting to me – a feeling that was not disabused by my two years as a junior reporter. However, after fifteen years of unproductive retirement as far as writing was concerned, I had little confidence in my ability to compete in what I knew to be a cutthroat world and it was with trepidation that I considered the chance of becoming a serious freelance journalist – it did not seem very likely that any editor would want to print something I wrote.

At this point my guardian angel decided to take a hand. An old friend from my newspaper days turned up running a Fleet Street news agency. He said that he would consider any features I sent him and then my problem was what to write about. After days of brain-cudgelling, I wrote a story about where and how to buy second-hand clothes in London, for at that time the second-hand clothes business was just beginning to boom. Some of the shops that sold them were very exclusive, specializing in clothes rumoured to have been thrown out by members of the royal family or by stage and film stars. One shop was stocked entirely with magnificent evening dresses – many of which had been worn on stage by Danny La Rue. My piece about those shops I called 'Second-Hand Rose' after a song popular at the time and a few days after I sent it to my friend, a cheque for £25 returned in the post. I was thunderstruck because £25 for an 800-word piece was a princely fee in those days – the going rate was around £8 to £10. My friend also said he would consider anything else I cared to send. In a flush of false optimism I saw poverty disappearing round the corner.

I began trekking all over London in search of stories for the agency. It has always been astonishing to me how nice people are when a journalist with a notebook turns up on their door-step and asks if they will be interviewed. Only sometimes did they even ask who I wanted to write the article for, and since the agency shared the name of a then popular publication which specialized in lesbian articles, I took care only to give my interviewees its initials and not its full name.

I interviewed people who won the 'Mastermind' contest; Army officers who took jobs as butlers; handwriting experts; a taxidermist who kept baby elephants and tiger cubs in his deep freeze and who specialized in stuffing tigers in snarling stances which were sold to tycoons to be chained to the legs of their desks, presumably to frighten off unwanted visitors. I interviewed the only female boxing promoter in Europe, who lived above a pub and had turned one of her rooms into a massive walk-in wardrobe for her 700 evening dresses and 30-odd wigs. I interviewed the man who made the Stetson hats worn by Paul Newman and Robert Redford in *Butch Cassidy and the Sundance Kid* and also a woman who made a living designing and selling Christmas cards for atheists.

The steady arrival of the news agency cheques bolstered my confidence and I decided to branch out. For years I had been an avid listener to 'Woman's Hour' and longed to be able to sell them a story. Anything I sent off, however, was smartly returned but one day I came across an idea that seemed better than average and I decided to phone the programme up – I couldn't face another rejection slip.

My guardian angel was working well that day because the girl who took my call said, 'Hold on a moment, I'll see what Mary thinks.'

Mary turned out to be Mary Redcliffe, a BBC producer who has become one of my most respected friends. She invited me up to Broadcasting House to talk to her about the idea and do a voice test – a voice test! I could hardly believe it. Nothing so exciting had happened to me for years and I looked forward to the appointment like a child looking forward to Christmas. On the day I was so nervous I could hardly stand and had to be given a stiff couple of gins by a friend before I had the courage to step into the hallowed marble portals in Portland Place, full of false and ginny confidence. Mary turned out to be warm, friendly and humorous and she must have spotted the effects of my gins because she took me to the canteen and filled me up with coffee. As soon as we began to talk I liked her very much and felt totally at ease with her. After the interview was over she sent me home with a job to do – 'Just write me a little piece,' she said.

On the bus home my confidence evaporated with the alcohol. I had blithely promised to write Mary a piece but what about? By the time I got off the bus I knew I was about to blow my only chance. I shut myself up in my bedroom where I kept my desk and typewriter and sat staring out of the window brooding about my own nerve in contacting 'Woman's Hour' and my inability to follow it up. Then I saw them – my two dogs, Ham and Phoebe, pottering back home from their daily foray to the grocer's shop half a mile away.

Ham was an aged, blind West Highland terrier and Phoebe a fat and greedy pug. Both of them were severely addicted to chocolate and Phoebe had discovered an unfailing source of supply from a kindly woman who served in a branch of the Express Dairy. The trouble was that they had to negotiate two main roads to get there and Phoebe, eager to share her good fortune with Ham, took it upon herself to guide him over the roads, crossing between the cars with stately assurance. Ham was the only dog to have a seeing eye dog.

One day I was browsing among the stacks of food in the Express Dairy when I heard a commotion at the cash desk. 'Poor little things, they must be starving,' said the cashier, handing Penguin biscuits to my dogs who wolfed them down with voracious delight. She then opened the door to allow them to waddle off again and the shop settled down to discuss the disgrace of someone keeping dogs and not feeding them properly. They decided that Ham and Phoebe belonged to a well-known pop singer who lived in the district and whose Afghan hound was also allowed to roam the streets. I slipped out, craven coward, hoping that Ham and Phoebe would not see me and and give me away.

The piece I wrote about that incident was amazingly accepted by 'Woman's Hour', and when it was eventually broadcast I was a split personality – half full of pride and half burning with shame at my Scottish accent and my faltering delivery. Listening to myself was a chastening experience but at last I was launched on a career and for the first time in years I was earning money by doing something that I really enjoyed.

A widowed friend, who has also taken up an interrupted career after her husband died, said recently, 'Since David died I have often been sad but I have never been bored.'

Looking back I agree that boredom has not been one of my problems either, in fact there have been times when a bit of ennui would not have come amiss. In a strange way, however, there has always been a sustained atmosphere of excitement and hope that has carried me on through my crises. The need to succeed is a tremendous spur.

When my work began to engross me, problems that would have reduced me to a weeping wreck previously could be more easily shrugged off. One afternoon my car, parked outside the house, was completely flattened by a branch blown off our tree. Philosophically I accepted the loss and bought myself an old banger that was the same model as the car Adam and I had used to go on honeymoon. When I opened the door the smell of its upholstery brought back a rush of memories and that was why I bought it. In fact it turned out to be a better investment than the car that was flattened because it ran for two years and was eventually sold for its purchase price.

When my work had sufficiently increased for me to be able to pay her, Mercy came to help in the house. She brought order into our domestic chaos and the furniture began to gleam again under her hand. I have never known anyone who could get through so much work in such a short time as she did. She said she liked working in our house because 'It's full of old junk, just like me granny's.' Mercy seemed to have contact with a large number of people who could supply her with things that 'fell off the back of a lorry'. Once she asked me 'Fancy some Vim, love?' and what I got was not a couple of cans but a whole case. She helped me to see that life could be funny again especially one afternoon when she had been spring-cleaning the kitchen. When I came home it was pristine and sparkling – all but one dust-encrusted vase on the top of the cupboard. Mercy saw my eye on it and she said:

'I didn't touch that one, love, you've got your husband in there, haven't you?'

We roared with laughter when I took the vase down to show her that the dust inside was only the ordinary household variety. Mercy's mistake routed my last awful memory of

Adam's bronze casket and it was a relief beyond describing to be able to laugh about it.

Little by little the links with the past were being cut. The day I voted for a political party that had been anathema to Adam I fully expected to be struck down by a thunderbolt as I left the polling booth. Then I sold his dining-room table – a purchase of which he was very proud – and spent the money on a trip to Russia by boat for myself and the children. When I returned I wrote a 'Woman's Hour' piece about it which began 'I sailed to Russia on my dining-room table . . .'

The house itself, which at first had seemed like a safe fortress, suddenly seemed to constrict me, to tie me back to times that had been and we made the decision to move. The big problem was where to go. With the children I spent hours pondering this but secretly I had already taken my decision – I was going back to the Scottish Borders where I had been brought up and which were, and continue to be, a kind of Utopia for me. Miraculously, after many false starts, we sold our house and at the same time I saw an advertisement in a Sunday newspaper for the house that sounded ideal . . . in fact, I thought I knew which one it was. When I phoned the owner, my hunch was proved correct and within a few weeks I had bought it.

In spite of taking a chance and moving away from London, my freelance career did not wither and die. I sell pieces to newspapers and magazines all over the world, and though I am very far from rich, I love my work and I very much love the place where I now live. By leaving London I moved into the second phase of my life; my marriage and my mourning are all now part of my memories.

# 9

# *Don't Shoot the Pianist*

One of the clichés of widowhood is 'You never forget': you do not forget, but you learn to remember without pain. That stage is reached when you find you have battled through to the 'clearing on the other side of the wood'.

One of the purposes in writing this book has been to attempt to chart some of the danger points along the way. It has also been therapeutic, because as I have worked through the evolution of myself from a widow to a woman on her own, the progress of events has fallen into a pattern. The memories have often been painful and I have been forced to look at things which I would have rather forgotten forever but, having brought them back into the light of day, by writing them down I feel as if I have at last routed all my old ghosts.

In no way do I feel that I have been an 'ideal widow'; in no way do I want to set myself up as an operational model for other people. I have made my mistakes, not once but many times. I have stepped into the pitfalls that I did not realize were there. What I do want to say however is that recovery *is* possible. It is certain that life can begin again no matter how grievously hurt you are by the death of someone who was all important to you. And once you begin to recover, you are being given the opportunity to remake your life, to build something new out of chaos, to find a new self-determination and a new philosophy. Looking back it seems as if my life has fallen into two distinct parts that are split off from each other by a Sunday in November. The second half is my own creation and, if it is good or bad, I have no one to praise or blame except myself.

The first thing that you must appreciate is the quality of happiness. Bertrand Russell wrote that to be without some of the things you want is an indispensable part of happiness. Nothing, not even the most perfect flower or the most painstaking picture, is ever perfect. It is the flaws that contribute towards realism and reality. True happiness is best appreciated once you have known what it is like to be very sad, to have the fringe memory of sadness pointing up the highest points of life.

Before Adam died, there were many, many times when I was happy but now it does not seem that I was immediately conscious of them. Now happiness is almost palpable. It has a concrete quality that makes me gasp with delight and I can feel it about the most minute things . . . a fine sunny morning with the dew silvering the grass and spiders' webs stretching across the branches of my plum tree can stop me in my tracks and I feel the stunning revelation of how happy I am, how lucky I am to be alive at that precise moment. It is a mistake to expect happiness to be continuous. You do not sully it by knowing that soon you may be sad again.

One of my earliest memories is of wandering in a grass field when I was very small – perhaps aged between two and three – with the fronds of grass branching above my head and the colours of wild flowers sparkling like jewels within reach of my hand. Yellow buttercups, pink-edged daisies, blue corn-flowers and scarlet poppies. It seemed to me that I was in some sort of heaven and even with my infant mind I realized that I was experiencing a transcendental happiness. The ability to give yourself over to happiness like that is childlike but it is something which can be developed again in adulthood and which can add infinitely to the quality of life. Recently I saw a painting by a nineteenth-century artist called Andrew Nicholl who specialized in pictures of Irish landscapes which he painted behind a foreground of wild flowers and grasses. His vision was the same as the one I remembered as a child and I was totally entranced by the picture and the knowledge that the artist had the same experience of bliss as I had myself.

It is not disloyal to the person who has died for the one who is left behind to seek and find new happiness. Nor is it disloyal for them to seek and find a new personality. Women in particular find this rebuilding essential if they are not to spend the rest of their lives as someone's 'widow'. In the first years of my new life, I found it necessary to explain myself to everyone – 'I'm a widow, my husband died . . .' It seemed impossible for me to have a place anywhere without a relevant tag, a link with some authoritative figure even if he was dead. Women have always been conditioned to accept a protected role, even those with the most eager need to have a personality of their own. It now seems that my inability to accept that someone somewhere was going to sort out my life again was a vestigial relic of that need for protection. When I began to accept that the someone who was going to sort my life out was *me*, recovery began. A few years ago, I suddenly realized that I had stopped explaining myself, I had stopped thinking of myself as Adam Taylor's widow. After we moved back to Scotland it no longer seemed relevant to tell people what I was and it came as a surprise when I heard that there was much speculation in the village about my exact status – was I divorced, separated, widowed or had I ever been married at all? One curious caller actually asked me the question. Far from being annoyed, I was flattered because it showed me how far I had travelled along my road to self-determination for now I did not feel the need to slip in my visiting card, 'I'm a widow'. I'm not a widow now, I'm a person in my own right.

This new person is not the same as the woman who was emotionally shattered by the news of her husband's death. The injunction to 'start your life again' ignores the fact that the restarting is often undertaken unconsciously, bit by bit you learn to make your own decisions. You learn not to repine or to look back in bitterness. You learn to value your friends in the sure knowledge that they belong to you and are not united to you by proxy.

You learn to mend the fuses because there is no one to whom you can hand the screwdriver and say, 'It's your job.' You learn to combat the depredations of tradesmen who think that solitary women are ripe for exploitation. In the beginning you suffer those injustices because you do not know how to stand up for yourself but the time comes when you stop thinking so little of yourself that you cannot fight back. With the growing confidence of being able to survive alone comes the ability to fight your own fights. You learn to look people in the eye, not aggressively but with confidence, and when you can do that you are well on the way to self-determination.

There are still women who never attempt to take on an active role in life – they are second-line figures all their lives and when widowhood comes to them it is almost insupportable. Perhaps one of the ways of learning to live as a widow is changing your way of living as a wife – learn to drive a car, do not always be content to sit as a passenger; learn to handle money; take an active share in the organizing of your married life; learn to have opinions. It is shocking to meet women who say, 'We never eat salads, my husband does not like them though I do.' They should share their likes and dislikes, allowance should be made for both prejudices.

Looking back I can see that I was a second-line wife. I stayed at home, dusted the furniture and looked after the children while inside I unconsciously wished for a chance to make something else of my life. Now, having been given that chance because of what seemed like a cataclysmic blow, I am able to admit that many aspects of my life have changed for the better. It seems like unnatural heresy to admit this but it is true.

I do not dust any more. If the house needs a drastic clean I can pay someone to do it for me and I am able to recognize that as a housekeeper I was a total failure. Domestic arrangements for me tend on the side of chaos and that is how I like them.

I eat what I like, when I like and where I like. I can stay in bed all day and work all night if I choose. My only priority is getting my work done and there is no one to tell me when I should do it. I can read in bed till four in the morning and I can listen to the World Service in the early hours without fear of disturbing the sleep of a husband who is the wage-earner of the family.

Above all, I can spend my own money. I have earned it all and if I choose to be improvident with it, the only explanation of my stupidity that I have to give is to myself. There is a heady satisfaction about spending your last pound on something you could well do without. If I had been sensible I would never have spent a legacy on a six-week trip across the Siberian wastes and down through China by train. There were far more sensible ways I could have invested the £2000, but it was a most marvellous experience and provided me with a tremendous amount of material to write about. If I were more sensible I would not run a two-seater car but a sensible, economical family saloon. If I were a sensible woman I would not buy paintings instead of insurance policies, a second-hand mink coat instead of an all-purpose mac.

As a memory of my past, I still have a cabin trunk of clothes beneath my bed. Those were my 'executive wife' garments – rustling cocktail dresses, a well-cut suit, shoes with gilt bars round the heels and even a couple of sensible hats. If I were to put clothes like that on now I would feel as if I was in fancy dress because in no way would they express my personality – perhaps they did not express it then either. Now I buy clothes that say something about me – sometimes I pay far more for them than I can afford and sometimes I buy them in second-hand shops. My best hat is a black velour trilby that I bought in a junk shop for £5; my wardrobe has two evening coats, one which cost me so much that I still blench when I think of it and another, equally fantastic, that I bought for £1 in a Dublin open market.

It is of absolutely no consequence to me what people think about my clothes and I am quite capable of going out to shop in a track suit, a fur coat, trailing scarves and my trilby. I love that hat. The junk shop owner told me he had bought it from the widow of a Jewish rabbi and I never saw its like until I watched George Burns in the film *The Sunshine Boys* – there he was, sporting my hat. It looked well on him too.

The Barrow poets have a wonderful poem in their repertoire – the musings of a middle-aged woman about how, as she grows older, she is more aware of the possibility of openly showing what she feels. She intends to be as outrageous as she can – spend all her pension on brandy and satin sandals or to sit down on the pavement 'whenever I feel tired to make up for the sobriety of my youth'. I am going to make up for the sobriety of my first life by allowing eccentricity to take over. I intend to go on filling my house with dogs, running my unsuitable car, wearing unsuitable clothes and saying exactly what I like for as long as I can. I'm not completely unconventional yet, but I'm trying.

Recovering from widowing can be compared to the feeling you get when blood starts flowing again into a numbed limb. It hurts at first but in the end the relief is enormous. It would be a lie if I denied that from time to time I feel very lonely and long for some sympathetic partner whom I could love and who would love me back. But I have the consolation of many loyal and trusted friends. Giving yourself up to loneliness is a terrible indulgence. What has to be done is to concentrate on its positive side. Living on your own does not automatically mean that you must be lonely, and the longer you live as a single entity, the more valuable your solitude becomes. It would now be insupportable for me to have to share every minute of my life with anyone else, no matter how much I loved them. Only by being alone can you learn to turn your thoughts inwards and to listen to yourself.

The cure for loneliness is not finding another lonely person to share it with you – that could in the end condemn both of you to greater sufferings. The cure instead lies in a reaching out from yourself to the outside world, an opening of your eyes that have for so long been looking down only at yourself and your sadness. The development of what is in every one of us and the knowledge that we all have something to communicate to others is the best gift that you can give to the world because it means that you have a genuine interest in the people around you. One old lady who lives a full and satisfying life on a small income was astonished when I asked if she had ever felt lonely – 'I've never been lonely in my life,' she said. Her prescription was to care about other people, to maintain contact with her family and friends, to invite them to see her and give them pleasure when they came, to be prepared to help them if help was needed and to listen to them when they were in trouble.

For a long time after Adam's death I would have been happy to have died too and the only link I had with life was my love and concern for my children. Now I am eternally grateful that my life did not end as well on that fateful Sunday because I would never have known what pleasures and pains lay ahead for me in the second life I have been given. There is a French saying that life is an onion which we peel in tears, but I prefer an even better one – also coined by a Frenchman, Rene Coty. He said, 'It is a pity to shoot the pianist when the piano is out of tune.'

The piano is badly out of tune when your life disrupts and you lose the person you have loved and on whom you have relied entirely. But throwing away or wasting the life that is left to you is a classic way of shooting the pianist. Gather yourself together, slowly perhaps and haltingly, but remember that even the most out-of-tune pianos can be made to play good music again.

# 10

⌘

# *What to Do when Someone Dies*

FIRST of all it is necessary to register the death with the local Registrar in the district in which the death has occurred. This address can be found in the local phone book under Registration of Births, Deaths and Marriages. In England and Wales this must be done within five days; in Scotland, however, eight days are allowed.

It is not necessary for a widow or widower to register the death personally; someone else can do it for them. However, certain documents must be presented – a medical certificate giving the cause of death; the deceased's medical card if possible; a coroner's certificate if applicable; the deceased's birth and marriage certificates.

The person registering the death should also know the deceased's address, full name (including maiden name), place and date of birth, occupation, and name and occupation of the spouse with the spouse's date of birth.

The registrar will then issue a certificate of registration of death; a certificate for burial or cremation which should be given to the funeral director, leaflets about widows' benefits and income tax.

There is no charge for this unless extra copies of the various certificates are needed.

Another thing to do after registering a death is to make (or remake) your own will. Only one person in three in the UK takes the trouble to make a will, and even if they have nothing much to leave this can cause terrible problems for families, especially where there are children involved.

The safest way to make a will is to do it through a lawyer; this need not be expensive because every so often, there is a national 'Make a Will' week when lawyers provide the service at low cost, which should be well under £100. Shop around among your local lawyers for the best price.

# 11

# *Useful Addresses and Information*

WHEN this book first appeared, the counselling craze was starting but since then it has got out of hand. Granted, there are situations which can be made easier by receiving help and advice from people who have suffered similar problems, but often the counsellors do not have that experience and are only driven by the need to participate in other people's lives and do 'good works'.

There are now people and organisations eager to counsel victims of any problem from the trivial to the traumatic. One victim of a minor burglary told me that she suffered more annoyance from the visits of over-eager counsellors after the incident than she had from the burglary itself. More seriously, after the Dunblane tragedy, many local people were upset and offended by the unwanted influx of counsellors into their small town. They actually appealed for them to go away.

The solution to surviving life's blows – and very few people can escape at least one of them – often lies in the individual's own hands. The first thing to do is work out exactly what your problem is and then tackle it or go for help to an appropriate place.

When *Living with Loss* first appeared, I sat on panels where members of the audience asked questions or added their opinions.

Many of them had genuine problems for which solutions could be found by doctors, lawyers, good friends or financial advisers, but there were others, a surprisingly high proportion, only eager to protest about how badly life had treated them and who did not really want any practical suggestions on what they could do about it. They were impossible to advise because they were looking for a fairy godmother who would wave her wand and say 'Abracadabra, it didn't happen. Your life will go back to what it used to be!' It was tempting to tell them the truth – wake up to reality, find a lover, get a job, start living a new life, but that was not what they wanted to hear.

There was no point uttering hackneyed maxims like 'You'll feel better soon', because life never goes back to what it once was and it is essential to move on and stop looking backwards. There are some problems that can be solved or made easier by sharing them – and frankly, some that cannot. Any counselling or helping agency that guides people in a positive, forward direction is to be congratulated but too often they only want people to 'talk about it' and that can be counter-productive.

The growth of the counselling industry has meant that compiling a comprehensive list of places to go for help today about any of the possible areas of trouble in widowhood is more or less impossible. A glance at the Yellow Pages will be enough to convince you that, like amateur gardening, using a pin to pick one's counsellor for a specific problem is probably as good a way as any.

There are, however, a few organisations that have stood the test of time, and their names follow:

AGE CONCERN, Astral House, 1268 London Road, London SW16 4ER. Tel: 0208 679 8000.

All aspects of welfare for the elderly. Good range of useful leaflets.

BENEFITS AGENCY. Listed in every telephone book and an invaluable source of information on Child Benefit, pensions and Social Security payments.

Social Security is a very complicated field and liable to change with every Budget but immediately following a husband's death, widows are at the moment given a tax-free lump sum providing they or their husband are under retirement age. In 1999 this stood at £1000 but this is liable to change in 2000. Note that the retirement age for women will be phased in from 60 to 65, as is the case with men, between 2010 and 2020.

Other benefits available include Child Benefit which is paid to people bringing up children on their own; Income Support is paid to people whose income is below a certain level (you do not receive Income Support if you are working more than 16 hours a week or have over £8000 in savings); Family Credit; Housing Benefit, which is help with rent for people with less than £16,000 in savings; and Council Tax Benefit for people on a low income.

Widow's pensions: At the moment women under the age of 45 do not qualify for widow's benefits unless they have dependent children and then they will receive a widowed mother's allowance. To check your claim ask for leaflet NP45 if you are over retirement age, or GL14 gives general information for men or women who are widowed.

CHARITY COMMISSION, Harmsworth House, 13–15 Bouverie Street, London EC4Y 8DP. Tel: 0870 333 0123. Website http://www.charity-commission.gov.uk.

Maintains an official list of all the 180,000-plus registered charities in England and Wales. An organisation can only be registered as a charity if it is set up to pursue legally charitable activities. The register can be viewed on the Internet website.

CITIZENS ADVICE BUREAU. Central Office: Myddelton House, 115–23 Pentonville Road, London N1 9LZ. Tel: 0207 833 2181. The Scottish association is a separate body and can be found at 26 George Square, Edinburgh EH8 9LD. Tel: 0131 667 0156.

A truly wonderful organisation with branches throughout the country – check under Counselling in the local Yellow Pages. Staffed by well-briefed volunteers who give advice about all sorts of problems and distribute a selection of useful leaflets. Especially helpful on employment, money and pension problems. The help given is free but funding is always a problem for the CAB which receives grants from the Department of Trade and Industry and local authorities.

CRUSE, 126 Sheen Road, Richmond, Surrey TW9 1UR. Tel: 0208 332 7227. Fax: 0208 332 3131.

Country-wide, with almost 200 branches, Cruse celebrated its 40th anniversary in 1999. It was founded in 1959 as a support group for young widows and their children by Mrs Margaret Torrie, who at the time of writing is still alive, but retired. In 1980 the work was extended to widowers as well as widows, and, in 1986, Cruse extended its services to all bereaved people, changing its name from 'The National Organisation for the Widowed and their Children' to 'Cruse Bereavement Care'.

As well as offering free direct help and advice, Cruse also promotes the needs of bereaved people to the Government.

INLAND REVENUE. Tax offices are listed under 'Inland Revenue' in every telephone book. Officers are prepared to give face-to-face advice. Tax is levied on Social Security payments but there is an extra tax allowance for widows and for people bringing up children on their own. They issue a leaflet IR91, 'A Guide for Widows'. Also IR92, 'A Guide for One-Parent Families'.

NATIONAL ASSOCIATION OF BEREAVEMENT SER-VICES, 20 Norton Folgate, London E1 6DB. Tel: 0207 247 1080.

A slightly chaotic organisation which co-ordinates services for the dying and bereaved throughout the UK. Formed in 1988 at a time when a series of disasters highlighted the need for a national co-ordinating body. Provides a telephone helpline.

NATIONAL ASSOCIATION OF WIDOWS, 54–7 Allison Street, Digbeth, Birmingham B5 5TH. Tel: 0121 643 8348.

Set up in 1971 as a 'widow-to-widow' service by the late Mrs June Hemer who felt that only a widow could hold the hand of another widow and say 'I have been there'. The Association now has branches throughout the country and it campaigns for widows' rights as well as offering them friendship and a better social life. It has a pen–club open to all widows, and maintains a contact list of all members who are interested in contacting others. There is no charge.

NATIONAL COUNCIL FOR ONE-PARENT FAMILIES, 255 Kentish Town Road, London NW5 2LX. Tel: 0207 428 5400.

Provides free written information for all lone parents. Free phone helpline. Free database search to advise people on how to contact their local services and other sources of support. Advice on child maintenance issues.

SAMARITANS. Headquarters: 10 The Grove, Slough, Berkshire SL1 1QP. Tel: 01753 216500, or look up 'Samaritans' in the phone book. E-mail: jo@samaritans.org, or anonymously on samaritans@anon.twwells.com.

Specially trained and selected listeners at the end of a telephone line for people in distress. There are 204 centres in the UK and Republic of Ireland and over 180 branches open 24 hours a day. Founded in 1953 by Chad Varah to provide free confidential, emotional support to people in distress. The organisation receives approximately 4.4 million calls a year.

# Index

# Index